"Anyone who thinks teenagers are immune to self-image issues doesn't know teenagers. But how many times do parents contribute to a teen's lack of confidence without even knowing it? Nicole O'Dell's practical suggestions and insightful advice help guide parents through the minefield of raising a self-assured yet godly adolescent. A great tool for anyone who cares about teenagers!"

—Melody Carlson, award-winning author of *Diary of a Teenage Girl* and *TrueColors*

"This series is the answer to the cry of my heart. It's wise, it's tactical, and it's preemptive. Among the huge selection of parenting books on my shelf, I've never had another one give me tingles and make me shout, 'Yes! This is it!' I feel empowered and inspired as a parent and have already implemented the strategies this series teaches."

—Jill Williamson, award-winning author of *By Darkness Hid* and the Blood of Kings trilogy

Hot Buttons Series

HOT BUTTONS

IMAGE EDITION

Nicole O'Dell

Kregel
Publications

Hot Buttons Bullying Edition
Copyright © 2013 by Nicole O'Dell

Published by Kregel Publications, a division of Kregel, Inc., P.O. Box 2607, Grand Rapids, MI 49501.

The author and publisher are not engaged in rendering medical or psychological services, and this book is not intended as a guide to diagnose or treat medical or psychological problems. If medical, psychological, or other expert assistance is required, please seek the services of your own physician or certified counselor.

ISBN 978-0-8254-4244-5

Printed in the United States of America

13 14 15 16 17 / 5 4 3 2 1

The Hot Buttons series, as a whole, is dedicated to my mom, who had to deal with more hot buttons when I was a teen than she'd care to remember. Also to my six children, who have so graciously provided the research I needed to write these books . . . whether I wanted them to or not. And to my husband, Wil, who somehow managed to make my teen years look like a walk in the park.

Hot Buttons Image Edition *is for all the young people who have wished they were someone else, and for the parents who love them.*

➤➤➤ *Too many people overvalue what they are not and undervalue what they are.*

—Malcolm S. Forbes

Contents

Part Four: Parent-Teen Study Guide

Image.

Sometimes I wonder why I didn't start with this subject as I began the Hot Buttons series. So much about choices and the power to make good ones comes from self-confidence. How a person feels about appearance, self-worth, social status, and everything else that contributes to one's self-image significantly impacts daily choices.

As we'll see as we move through this book, the image I've had of myself over the years has contributed to both my poor choices and my good choices. Some experiences early on led me down a road of destructive choices that were fueled by a poor self-image. I wanted so badly to be accepted by my peers and valued by others, and I didn't believe I had inherent worth, so I succumbed to peer pressure and pursued popularity at all costs.

As I've worked on this book, I've prayed that my heart would be transparent and that I'd be able to convey what the Lord has shown me as I've walked this road both as a teenager and as a parent. I want only to share the truth and pass along the information parents need to hear, and then give you the tools you need to talk to your tweens and teens about these issues and to make a difference in their lives.

As parents of these wonderful creatures God has entrusted to us, we want so badly for them to see themselves as He does, and as we do. So how can we make that happen when the world is constantly shouting that they aren't good enough? That's what we're here to uncover.

As I've shared in each Hot Buttons book, the game of Scenarios came about years ago when I was searching for ways to lead my children to make good decisions. I decided it would be far better to talk to them proactively about issues they would one day face, than it would be to wait until they were buried under the consequences of their poor choices—like I was.

I knew I'd have to be willing to talk about the tough subjects like sex, drugs, alcohol, addictions, dating, and pornography, perhaps even before they actually knew what those things were. If I had any hope of being as proactive as I wanted to be, no subject could be off-limits and nothing could be ignored.

That's significantly more difficult with the issue of self-image because it's rooted in the most subtle lies. Combating the lies of the enemy isn't easy, but we can do it!

The practice of Scenarios became a favorite activity in my home and proved invaluable in preparing my teens to make good choices. The best part was the talks we'd have after the choices were made and the consequences were presented. My children felt free to explore, ask questions, safely experiment with the options—and then, when similar scenarios came up in real life, they were prepared to make the right choices.

The Hot Buttons series was birthed as a way for you, Mom and Dad, to bring those principles and practices into your home. You'll find each hot-button issue covered in detail with warning signs and recommendations laid out in simple form. Then, you'll find the Strategic Scenarios, which will enable you to approach your teens with these topics and give them the same opportunity to make the safe discoveries that I gave my kids.

And I trust you'll see the same results I have.

Acknowledgments

Thank you so much, Kregel Publications, for embarking on this amazing project with me. I can't thank you enough for your trust in me and for allowing me to work on these vital tools that will help parents guide their tweens and teens to make victorious choices.

I want to thank those special friends of mine who know just what to say when I'm feeling nervous or inadequate. Cynthia Gramm, you top the list. Your encouragement means the world to me.

To my Savior, Jesus Christ, thank You for the love You lavish on me that has pulled me from the pit of my own image issues. Without the work You continue to do in my heart and life, I'd never have been able to share this message with readers, let alone even come close to seeing myself the way You do.

PART ONE

Image
HOT
BUTTONS

What exactly is a hot-button issue?

It's one of those topics people generally acknowledge to be inflammatory or controversial. It's a real issue that hits hard and is often confusing—one that can be life-changing and often requires immediate attention.

My goal in writing these Hot Buttons books is to face these topics now, together, so you can walk your kids through the necessary prep work, rather than ignore the issues and wait until they pop up sometime down the road when you'll have to react. You have the parental right and the godly responsibility to hit these issues hard, head-on, preemptively instead of simply reacting to the challenge-of-the-day. Once your teenager brings a subject up to you or you find out it's a problem, you've missed the opportunity to lay the foundation on that topic. Someone else already did it for you. Don't allow that to happen.

Prepared:
Answering *Why*

Image. Body image. Self-esteem. Don't you get kind of tired of all the focus on this subject, which does nothing but turn a person's attention inward? *How do I look? What am I worth? Where do I fit in with the rest of the world? Am I good enough?*

God answers all of those questions in His Word, but today's youth culture is rabidly desperate to hear the answers from its peers. The tweens and teens of today aren't willing to take God's word for it, or our word for it—after all, what do parents know? So we have to be intentional about speaking a healthy, godly self-esteem into our kids' lives. We need to make it happen for them. We need to equip our kids to ward off the attacks of the enemy designed to keep them filled with insecurity, because that insecurity will cripple their effectiveness for the kingdom of God.

Each flicker of self-doubt, each instant the enemy robs your teenager of joy or zeal, can be countered with some level of preparation—whatever groundwork we've laid in our kids' lives. In those moments, these are the resources our children have to pull from. That preparation cannot be ramped up in the heat of the moment. In that instant, their commitment is what it is and there's no more time to gird it up. They're on their own with whatever tools we've already given them.

That might sound harsh, but the world is a harsh reality of comparison and not-good-enoughs. And amid the pursuit of popularity or the clamor for approval, it's difficult to raise wise, godly teenagers who are willing to deny themselves confidence or security in the social realm. If you're in the process of raising tweens or teens, you probably already know that it's rare for kids to get a healthy grasp on their image without guidance. You likely are dealing with either an overinflated or an undervalued sense of self.

Each extreme carries its own set of concerns. Bringing a teenager down from an inflated ego is a challenge. It's important to break the selfishness without breaking the spirit. You don't want to hurt the good parts in the process. On the other hand, overcoming a negative self-image is not an easy battle and it's a personal one I still fight to this day. But there are ways to reshape it and to overcome its effects.

Dispel the myth of effective insulation.

Do you ever wish you lived in a Christian bubble, able to completely insulate your children from the world? As much as that would make life easier for us in the short term, it would result in teens who are sent out into the world unarmed and unprepared for situations they won't be able to avoid forever. Visualize a scene in which an adolescent steps from a time machine into a war zone. If they enter the fray with no preparation or skills, they'll fall.

Our kids will face temptation, peer pressure, and self-esteem issues in their schools, hanging out with friends, and even at their churches. This is a fact. Since we know what they'll face, isn't it more important to prepare them for good choices with a solid foundation, than it is to attempt to create a sterile, pressure-free environment in a world that makes it impossible?

If you're at all like me, you wish you could walk with your kids through the battles of life—guarding and guiding them through each pressure-filled moment, each decision between right and wrong, each temptation. You wish you could stand in for them until they are mature enough to see and appreciate the big picture. But, while we absolutely should have high expectations and maintain a tight grip on the reins as we raise our families, we also need to prepare our kids to stand alone, to be strong in the face of temptation.

Nothing we do can fully protect our kids from the powerful combination of peer pressure plus insecurity. You can, however, affect how prepared they are to defend themselves against the onslaught. In each and every pressure-filled moment of decision, there comes a point—just before the final decision is made—when all the preparation, forethought, and wisdom we've been equipping our kids with comes to a head. In the heat of the moment, they make a choice based on all the work that came before. Our teens need to be equipped to make the right choice; armed with something more than *no*; braced by facts, your wisdom, and God's Word.

Take the mystery out of sin!

The early years are for training our children. In Mark 14:38 we're warned to watch and pray about temptation. The spirit might be willing to avoid

Prepared: Answering *Why*

it, but the body is weak. How much more so for someone who isn't prepared for the temptation! We may have raised the most well-intentioned kids on the planet—ones whose spirits are willing—but their flesh is weak. They need to be trained.

> Therefore you shall **lay up these words of mine in your heart and in your soul**, and bind them as a sign on your hand, and they shall be as frontlets between your eyes. You shall **teach them to your children**, speaking of them when you sit in your house, when you walk by the way, when you lie down, and when you rise up. (Deut. 11:18–19 NKJV)

Why does it matter? Why put so much focus on guarding your kids against the pursuit of popularity and a good self-image? What's in it for them if they stand on God's Word in the face of peer pressure, risking friendships, popularity, good times? They need to care about what God has called them to do. A line from my favorite worship song says, "Break my heart for what breaks yours. . . ." That isn't makeup, trendy clothes, and a perfect body. Only a time-invested parent, who prays as much as she talks and listens as much as she prays, will raise a teenager who can see past the mirror and the celebrity gossip to the heart of Christ.

What tools will they need? Our teens and preteens need truth. And they need a life filled with wholesome things like church activities and sports—rather than too much time home alone riddled with boredom or too much time with outside influences like the wrong kinds of friends and the media. They need to be a part of a family that is serving the Lord, and watching parents who practice what they preach. They need to continuously grow in the knowledge of the Word and in relationship with God.

And they need to be prepared for the backlash that inevitably comes from saying no: persecution, disappointment, and even out-and-out rejection when they choose to stand for what's right. Children need to reach their teen years already armed with the tools necessary to make the hard choices—willing to withstand and endure persecution for the sake of Christ. Willing to walk alone if that's what He asks them to do.

What's the next step? They need you to walk with them, hand in hand, step by step. Mom, Dad, Guardian—they need you to be aware of what's going on. They need you to know them well. This requires time, communication, and godly, prayerful insight into the hearts and minds of your teens.

We can be confident parents, even in these scary times!

When we recognize that our kids struggle against a forceful current of media influence, self-esteem battles, and lies from the enemy, it's very difficult not to panic that they'll be swept away. We love them so much; we see such beauty and worth in them—it's hard to imagine they can't see it and might be more inclined to listen to strangers than to us.

We do have a promise to cling to, though.

> **Being confident of this**, that he who began a good work in you will carry it on to completion **until the day of Christ Jesus**. (Phil. 1:6)

Prepared: Answering *Why*

Let's break that down.

Being confident of this:
You can be sure that this is the way it is. It's a promise.

He who began:
Who began it? "He" did. Not you. Not your teen. God started . . .

A good work:
The work He started is a good and righteous thing.

Will carry it on to completion:
It will be finished. He didn't start something only to see it fall to pieces because of some teenage mistakes. It will be completed. It's a promise of God, and I choose to believe Him.

Until the day of Christ Jesus:
Every one of us, including our teens, is a work in progress. This work, which will be completed, has a long way to go . . . until the day of Christ Jesus, to be exact.

Protecting, shielding, and preparing our teens for life's hot-button issues isn't as black-and-white as a physical battle in which the wins and losses can be easily quantified. Self-esteem involves internal matters of the heart that we may struggle to identify. We must often blindly face the battles for our kids, operating more on faith than on sight, being obedient to the call of Christ and reliant on the leading of the Holy Spirit. In fact, we're told in Ephesians 6:12 that our struggle isn't even "against flesh and blood, but against the rulers, against the authorities, against the powers of this dark world and against the spiritual forces of evil in the heavenly realms."

As Christian parents, we need to insulate our families from negative outside influences. We should be watching over the words and images that enter our children's young minds through television, movies, and the like; and we need to be standing, ready to jump in with help the moment we see signs of danger. Our purpose is not to raise naive, uninformed wimps, but to safeguard our kids from the wiles of the enemy who whispers lies into their young, eager minds.

We have been given tools in God's Word to prepare us to guard against the confusion of this world. And we're granted partnership with the Holy Spirit, who will lead and guide us according to godly wisdom and insight. That guidance is invaluable as we prepare our kids for their popularity struggles, their body-image woes, and the quest for their personal identities.

CHECK POINTS ▶▶▶

CHECK POINTS

✓ The tweens and teens of today aren't willing to take God's word for it, or our word for it—after all, what do parents know? So we have to be intentional about speaking a healthy, godly self-esteem into our kids' lives. We need to make it happen for them.

✓ We need to equip our kids to ward off the attacks of the enemy designed to keep them filled with insecurity, because that insecurity will cripple their effectiveness for the kingdom of God.

✓ Our kids will face temptation, peer pressure, and self-esteem issues in their schools, hanging out with friends, and even at their churches. This is a fact. Since we know what they'll face, isn't it more important to prepare them for good choices with a solid foundation, than it is to attempt to create a sterile, pressure-free environment in a world that makes it impossible?

✓ "Break my heart for what breaks yours. . . ." That isn't makeup, trendy clothes, and a perfect body. Only a time-invested parent, who prays as much as she talks and listens as much as she prays, will raise a teenager who can see past the mirror and the celebrity gossip to the heart of Christ.

✓ Children need to reach their teen years already armed with the tools necessary to make the hard choices—willing to withstand and endure persecution for the sake of Christ. Willing to walk alone if that's what He asks them to do.

✓ Self-esteem involves internal matters of the heart that we may struggle to identify. We must often blindly face the battles for our kids, operating more on faith than on sight, being obedient to the call of Christ and reliant on the leading of the Holy Spirit.

Watchful:
Answering *When*

If your kids haven't reached the tween years yet, great! You are just in time to make a proactive difference, before the claws of comparison latch onto the hearts and minds of your kids. Ideally, the process of building an appropriate, healthy self-image into our kids would begin from birth: we'd avoid focusing on how cute, pretty, beautiful, handsome, athletic, or popular our kids are, and focus instead on the valuable things they do. "You acted like such a good friend just then." "That was great sharing." "You're so honest." But, sadly, so much of those early years are focused on cuteness—pictures, hairdos, darling outfits, and more.

I share a bit of my story in *Hot Buttons Bullying Edition*, and I'm sharing some of it here, too, because it absolutely applies to self-esteem, body image, and the pursuit of popularity.

The summer before I entered middle school, I went to Bible camp, where I got bit by a mosquito, from which I contracted encephalitis. That mosquito changed my life. It threw my thyroid and hypothalamus out of whack so that I was virtually unrecognizable in a very short period of time. I started junior high nearly twice the person I was when the summer started.

Day one of junior high:

I knew I was in for it. Entering that school felt like walking up to a hangman's noose. Dread descended upon me with each step.

At first, nothing happened; no one said a word to me. Then I discovered why. Most of the kids didn't recognize me. Until my name was called during attendance. I heard a few snickers, and then a boy I'd known my whole life called me *Butterball*. In front of everyone.

The ensuing months were horrifying. I was bullied in every sense of the word, and I hated trying to get through the day at school. I tried to pretend I was sick so I could stay home, or injured so I could avoid gym class where we had to change into gym shorts and do ridiculous things like climb a rope.

I was lucky, though: I had a couple of good friends who stuck beside me, and I was involved in my youth group at church, so I wasn't home, bored, and lonely. But I was hurting.

Things change very fast in the life of a teenager, however.

The summer before I entered high school, I went through puberty with a vengeance, and the hormonal shift threw my body back into working order, at least to a degree. I went on a major diet and added in a ton of exercise . . . and I started high school at an average weight.

Day one of high school:

That boy who had called me *Butterball* hit on me, and I fell for it. I didn't hold him accountable for his mistreatment of me. I didn't demand better for myself.

Several things that happened in this situation should have signaled the oncoming forest fire that would consume me, but both my parents and

I trusted too much in my previous personality, intellect, and wisdom. In hindsight, this progression could have been noticed:

- **Spark**: The weight gain and the subsequent signs that I was afraid to go to middle school.
- **Flicker**: The bullying.
- **Flame**: Extreme weight loss, diet, exercise—signs of a focus on appearance.
- **Blaze**: Attention paid to appearance and boys—even to the point of excusing their mistreatment of me.

What don't your teens want you to know?

It's uncomfortable to admit to feeling inadequate, unloved, ugly, afraid, or any other undesirable trait. Tweens and teens can barely identify those feelings, let alone talk about them. Discussing them voluntarily is an even more unlikely scenario. I know it was impossible for me.

That insecurity, coupled with peer pressure and a longing for approval, is the battleground where the enemy drives a wedge between truth and lie. Lies about self-worth are easy to believe, so that's where teens typically fall. But when they do—supposing that they recognize their failure—it's not likely that they're going to admit the truth to you. "I used vulgar language at school to impress the popular girls." "I went too far physically with George because he didn't make me feel fat." Saying it out loud sounds ridiculous and self-centered—but the feelings are real and compelling.

Watchful: Answering *When*

Knowing that they probably aren't going to spell it out for you, it's vital that you're educated about what your teens are exposed to, armed with the tools to guide them, and then ready to stand watch.

How early is too early?

Since the media and society are throwing pressure, expectations, and unrealistic ideals at your kids at incredibly young ages, you need to go after those tough issues even earlier than you think. You have to be willing to tackle tough issues like modesty, body image, celebrity influences, and self-esteem openly and honesty before any problems actually arise. You'll see, through this and all of the Hot Buttons books, why earlier is far better than later.

Let me ask you some questions:

- Does your child worry about what peers think?

- Has your tween or teen had a boyfriend or girlfriend?

- Has your child expressed concern or interest in popularity?

- Is there any focus on trendy clothing?

- Is your child unique or identified in some way that might be perceived as a weakness?

- Has your child experienced bullying? (See *Hot Buttons Bullying Edition* for more help on this one.)

- Are any of the above true for any of your child's close friends?

If you answered yes to any of those questions, even the last one, it may already be too late for the kind of preemptive strike I'm talking about, and you'll be doing a bit more of a reactive strike—which is equally necessary, as is ongoing follow-up. Don't misunderstand; I'm not saying that all of the checklist items are necessarily bad things. But they are clues into what your kids are thinking and about issues you need to address. Now.

How old is old enough?

Everyone is different. Some tweens are early bloomers who are far more advanced and aware of their identity and social status earlier than others of the same age. Then there are those who prefer to hang back in their childhood a little longer. In general, kids surrounded by older teens discover and experiment with popularity and peer pressure at a faster rate than those who are not.

Physical and emotional changes often go hand in hand, but not always at the same rate. Just because a young woman's body is capable of bearing children doesn't mean her mind is capable of mature decisions. Just because a boy has a man's body and a man's voice doesn't mean his head has caught up with the expectations and responsibilities that go along with being a man.

There is a clear distinction between puberty and adolescence. *Puberty* is physical. The effects are ones we can witness as maturing bodies transform. These changes start at different times for each individual and span several years.

The changes of *adolescence*, however, are more emotional and mental. Even though the physical adjustments suggest that emotional changes are imminent, they don't always go right along the same path with the same speed. So it's the hidden, stealthy nuances that you need to watch out for. They often reveal themselves in the pursuit of physical perfection and the desire for popularity that then drives the preteen or teenager to make unfortunate choices.

Can't I just wait it out?

It might be tempting to just wait and let the self-esteem stuff work itself out. High school doesn't last forever, and each stage of life brings its own concerns, so unless there's a red flag, why bother?

Waiting until your kids are in the heat of the peer pressure moment or suffering under the weight of self-doubt or worse, and expecting your teens to know how to handle something they haven't prepared for . . . well, it just might be too late. Instead, choose to prepare them well enough to save them from the mistakes and the pain that bad choices inevitably cause.

You have to be willing to tackle tough issues openly and honestly before they actually come up. That might feel uncomfortable when it comes to issues of image since you don't want to put ideas into their heads—like you're giving your preteen or teen too much information, maybe even more fodder for self-doubt where there was none. But you'll see, through the course of this and all of the Hot Buttons books, why it's not too early.

These days, young people are forced to make adult decisions and deal with adult problems long before we think they'll have to and long before they're ready. Since we don't expect the issues to come up so soon, we avoid them, and since our kids have no idea what looms on their horizon, they make mistakes out of simple lack of knowledge and preparation. We need to help them predetermine what their choices will be, rather than expect them to think clearly in the heat of those pressure-filled moments about an issue they haven't prepared for. It's far easier—and usually much more fun—to give in to peer pressure rather than to walk away. We need to strengthen them, through repeated doses of information and daily exercise, to walk away.

CHECK POINTS ▶▶▶

Watchful: Answering *When*

CHECK POINTS

✓ Insecurity, coupled with peer pressure and a longing for approval, is the battleground where the enemy drives a wedge between truth and lie. Lies about self-worth are easy to believe, so that's where teens typically fall.

✓ Knowing that they probably aren't going to spell it out for you, it's vital that you're educated about what your teens are exposed to, armed with the tools to guide them, and then ready to stand watch.

✓ Physical and emotional changes often go hand in hand, but not always at the same rate. Just because a young woman's body is capable of bearing children doesn't mean her mind is capable of mature decisions.

✓ Waiting until your kids are in the heat of the peer pressure moment or suffering under the weight of self-doubt or worse, and expecting your teens to know how to handle something they haven't prepared for . . . well, it just might be too late.

✓ Since we don't expect the issues to come up so soon, we avoid them, and since our kids have no idea what looms on their horizon, they make mistakes out of a simple lack of knowledge and preparation.

Proactive:
Answering *How*

In examining my own background through the clear view of hindsight, we identified the progression of friction that led to a blazing fire in my life. Let's break that down a bit. What could have been done at each stage of that growing fire to keep it from building?

Spark: The weight gain and the subsequent signs that I was afraid to go to middle school.

At this point, a parent would need to be on the lookout, realizing that it would be nearly impossible for a change such as the one I endured *not* to have an effect on self-perception and on the responses I expected from others. It was middle school after all. The worst place on the planet to go through something like that. Anticipating the potential problems could have paved the way to some great preparatory conversations while my heart was still open to them.

Flicker: The bullying.

My parents were unaware that any bullying was going on. Why? Because I was humiliated. It was mortifying enough just to endure, let alone to have to speak the words to someone else. At this point, a parent would need godly insight to anticipate the kinds of things that were likely to happen. Delicately posed questions, eyes wide open, and a lot of prayer for wisdom would have served Mom and Dad well in uncovering my struggles. If they had known what was happening at the time, they could have addressed it before it went further.

Flame: Extreme weight loss, diet, exercise—signs of a focus on appearance.

My frenzied approach to making a change, the tears I shed when I could fit into a pair of jeans from a regular store, the exuberance I showed when I could button shirts I previously had to wear loose and open . . . those were signs that I was struggling. The speed with which I dropped the weight, the change in my eating habits, the amount of exercise I did . . . further red flags. None of those are necessarily bad individually, but as a package and coupled with what I'd already experienced, it would have been reason to do some work.

Blaze: Attention paid to appearance and boys—even to the point of excusing their mistreatment of me.

My parents didn't know what I was experiencing, so they had no way of knowing that I was demonstrating a lack of self-respect, but perhaps if one of the earlier stages had been dealt with differently, hindsight being perfect, of course, I'd have handled this one differently too. As it turned out, I was so desperate for approval that when my bullies were ready to offer that approval . . . any girl in my position would have lapped it up any way she could. And I did. At this point, my parents could have realized that I was being dropped into the world of peer pressure and popularity without a parachute. I wasn't prepared because my previous years were spent dealing with different concerns. I needed help. More on this later . . .

Whatever you do, don't relate.

In that dark period of my life, it felt like no one had ever gone through exactly what I was facing. I was sure that no one had ever faced a similar struggle, so I would have never received help from someone who said something like, "I know what you're going through." You'll quickly lose credibility with your teens if you try to pretend you've had the same experiences. They don't want to hear that, and they won't believe it anyway.

Furthermore, they don't want you to be their friends. You're an adult with adult responsibilities, and you're at a time in your life when you're ready to face them. How can a teenager be expected to believe that you're a contemporary, a buddy, a friend? Studies have shown that teens feel the most distance from parents who try to be their friends. They have peers at school. At home, they need and want a parent.

This applies heavily to the issue of image. The quickest way to get your tween or teen to stop talking is for you to try to get her or him to open up under the guise of girl talk or guy talk. They will see right through that and you will lose their trust. They want a parent, not a BFF.

Instead of trying to relate and be accepted by your teen as a contemporary, gain credibility by admitting and embracing your differences.

What Not to Wear

Dress and modesty are very important to the issues of self-esteem, body image, and all the choices that go along with those things. How do your teenagers dress? What do they respond to in the appearance of others? How important are designer brands or trends to your kids? When you answer those questions honestly, you'll have some insight into what they might struggle with in the future.

Parents, you're going to want to set firm boundaries about the clothing choices your teens make, so it's necessary that you're a good role model. Your teens don't want you to dress like them—they just want you to blend in with the other parents. Make your teenager proud by dressing nicely and caring about your appearance, but don't take it so far that you're sharing clothes and trying to fit in with your teenagers and their peers. They don't want you digging in their closets or borrowing their shoes. Be confident and stylish, but stay toward the middle of the pack. Trying to be too trendy is as glaring a faux pas as being frumpy and out of date. Either extreme will be a source of embarrassment and a reason for her or him to feel distanced from you, which will cause a shutdown on the subject.

They want to be individuals—and they want to be proud of you, not have to compete with you. This is obviously truer for girls than boys, but, Dads, be sure you're supporting this need in your family.

Again, teenagers want to know their parents have a handle on life. If you're still floundering for your own identity and fighting to regain your youth, you're going to confuse your kids. Confidence, self-assuredness, and a moderate sense of style will make you more of a cool, yet dependable parent than if you wore a wardrobe straight out your teen's closet.

What Not to Say

In dealing with your kids' self-esteem and body image, you need to pray that God would give you wisdom to find just the right words to say. Well-meaning but ill-chosen phrases have been haunting people for generations. My dad used to call me plump. He thought it was a sweet, cute word to use that would take the sting away from thinking I was fat. But rather than hearing a different adjective to describe the same thing, I needed to have my focus turned to something else entirely.

The list of what not to say could go on forever, and it will be different for each child, so I'm going to recommend generalities:

- Pray that God would close your mouth if hurtful things are about to escape.
- Watch for clues about words and ideas that disappoint your child.
- Learn from other parents.
- Say nothing if you don't know what to say.
- Offer a hug to soothe tears when words seem hollow.
- Praise inner beauty over outer—and not just when it's your only choice.

There are also some validating phrases that can go a long way toward bridging the gap between you and your teens in general. (We'll get into specifics on the issues in later chapters.)

"Wow. I can see why this would be a confusing situation for you."

"Ouch. That must have really hurt."

"Would you like advice, or do you want me to just listen?"

"That must be so frustrating."

Proactive: Answering *How*

Whatever you do, don't be unapproachable.

One of the biggest issues leading to the demise of a parent's approach-ability is the lack of time. When asked what teens don't like about adults, the biggest complaint is that parents don't really take the time to listen. If parents aren't listening, and kids feel alone, of course they're going to look elsewhere for guidance—the media, their friends, and celebrities.

Below, I've listed some actual responses I received from teens when I asked them how they felt about communicating with their parents:

> "They pretend to hear by grunting, nodding, even sort of laughing when they think they should, but offer no real response to show me they even heard what I said."

> "They don't ask any questions about what I said. They're too happy I stopped talking and are afraid to 'put another quarter in' [a phrase that parent actually uses]."

> "Dad gets mad when I'm confused and just wants to spout out advice and expects me to take it without any further discussion."

> "They're 'too busy.'"

> "They say things like, 'Give me ten more minutes' or 'Not now, okay?' They aren't exactly rude, but they kind of brush me off."

"I know my mom loves me, but I just wish I could have a little face time for real."

Ouch.

Before you're going to be able to make an impact regarding your teenager's body and self-esteem issues, you're going to need to gain trust. They cannot ever feel that you're bored by their concerns. And much worse than them thinking you're bored is if they feel you're uninterested. If your teen thinks you just want her to go away, she will.

This is especially true when we're covering the issues that go along with image. Would it be helpful or detrimental to building a healthy self-esteem if a teenager felt insignificant to Mom or Dad? If you are too busy to languish over this subject with your teens, you're sending a message that it's really not all that important, and neither are they. And this is when the enemy sneaks in with lies about unworthiness, ugliness, and more.

Whatever you do, don't preach.

If raising children were simple, we'd be able to tell our kids how wonderful they are, and they'd believe us. They would see us as interesting, protective, and wise. They would cling to the sage advice and suggestions we put forth . . . in fact, they would beg for it.

But every parent knows that's just not the way it works. We didn't treat our parents that way (and probably still don't), and our kids won't see us in that light either. Most preteens will pretend to listen just long enough to make Mom and Dad happy, and then take their self-doubts and insecurities off to sob in private.

Like you and I did.

We believe wholeheartedly that God's Word, hidden in the hearts of believers—our children—will guide them through life's tough choices and difficult moments. We know it will reveal the truth about who they are, about the magnitude of their value. *We* believe it. *We* know it because we've had a long journey of learning from mistakes. But how will *they* know it until they experience it?

In other words, how do we get our teens to care about God's Word now, so they are armed and ready later when faced with hot-button issues? If we can't just wait and let our kids figure it out in their own timing, and we can't just tell them the way it is and leave it at that, then we need to find another way to get results.

Instead, speak truth with love and respect.

No matter how much you study or how passionate you become about the nuggets of truth you uncover in the Word, if you don't hand it down to your teens in love, it's meaningless. Scripture should never be used to attack, browbeat, or belittle. You should never, ever use Scripture to make your teen feel bad about his or her body, abilities, or overall self-worth. You see, over the years I've learned the hard way that knowledge spewed without love just sounds hollow.

> **If I speak in the tongues of men or of angels**, but do not have love, I am only a resounding gong or a clanging cymbal. If I have the gift of prophecy and **can fathom all mysteries** and all knowledge, and if I have a faith that can move mountains, **but do not have love, I am nothing**. (1 Cor. 13:1–2)

The message of Scripture will never reach our teens if they have a knowledge of the *content* of the Bible without a grasp of the intent—the love. And without the proper *context*, its message and power will never reach our teens. It cannot be simply a rule book. It's far too easy to rebel against rules. It must be a love letter.

It's not as easy as just handing down the facts and expecting our kids to soak them up like sponges. It simply doesn't work that way. Teens can tell if you've really taken the Scriptures to heart and applied them to your own life, or if you're just trying to do your spiritual duty by passing the doctrine—the fire extinguisher—on to them. They can tell if you're preaching out of control and fear, or if you're reaching out to them out of love and concern. Make sure the Bible is a part of each and every discussion you have about the choices your teens will make. That way, they'll understand that you're passing along God's Word, rather than coming at them with a because-I-said-so attitude.

Here are a few questions to ask yourself:

> Have you prayed over your kids' self-esteem before bringing it up?

> Are you taking biblical ideals and making them relevant issues for a teen? Are you being sensible in your approach?

> Are you using too many personal examples or lectures to which your teen can't, or doesn't want to, relate?

> Does your teen feel free to ask questions? Are you prepared to give or to find an answer if he or she does? Is there any subject that's taboo?

> Are you just handing down advice, or are you offering practical alternatives?

If we don't take the time to prayerfully pass down biblical truth and godly expectations in a contemporary way that appeals to our kids, then we can't fault them for not receiving those truths and expectations from us. Our babies come into the world fully trainable. We can't let go and expect them to teach themselves, because they will look for a source of education. It's your job to make sure you're the one providing it.

Instead, model by making right choices.

Here's the tough part, Mom and Dad. Do you live in such a way that you are above reproach on this issue? How can we ask our teenagers, who are far less prepared to deal with life's temptations than we are, to make good decisions if we're not modeling the difficult behaviors in front of them? How can we expect them to overlook our shortcomings and choose better for themselves? When things get tough, you'd better believe that they'll use our failures as excuses to justify their own.

Mom—and I speak to myself on this one, too—are you a crash dieter? Are you a yo-yo dieter? In chapters 6 and 7, you'll see the effects that can have on your tween and teen girls *and* boys.

To have the best life for your teen, you need to be living a righteous life yourself. In 1 Corinthians 9, Paul writes to the church about just this topic. He warns against preaching the truth to others but living in such a way that you miss it yourself:

Therefore **I do not run like someone running aimlessly**; I do not fight like a boxer beating the air. No, I strike a blow to my body and make it my slave **so that after I have preached to others, I myself will not be disqualified for the prize**. (vv. 26–27)

Be honest about your struggles and temptations—let your teens know that it isn't simple for you either. Be open about the cost of doing the right thing so they'll know they're on the right path. Imagine when you were a teen. If your parent had said to you at the right time, "You know what? I struggled with my body and with popularity when I was a teenager, too," wouldn't you have been more open to hearing from that parent on that tough subject?

If you pretend you were someone you weren't, you might tip the scales in the wrong direction as your teen is unable to relate to you and your supposed choices. It helps when teenagers can see their parents as human beings with weaknesses, failures, and struggles. They don't feel so alone in the battle.

So . . . share or don't share?

Don't worry, it's not a contradiction. It's just about wisdom and method. Taking every conflict, concern, or temptation your teen feels and turning the conversation into a tale about you and your own past is unwise and actually self-centered. But there is a right way to share from your past.

Proactive: Answering *How*

Some guidelines for sharing your past:

> ➤ Pull out choice nuggets from your history to punctuate the here and now—don't share everything that might relate. Be choosy.

> ➤ Keep your teenager as the focus, making the connection relevant to the issue at hand. Don't rabbit trail.

> ➤ Watch for cues of annoyance or disregard. If you sense your teen is tuning out, ask a direct question about the specific issue at hand. Bring the focus back to the moment.

> ➤ Tell a short story and make your relevant connection and then wait for follow-up questions. If your teen asks, feel free to answer. Otherwise, return the focus to the present.

Instead, provide "real life" practice.

If only we could simply horrify our kids with our own stories and impact their choices by what we went through. We'd share what we learned, and they'd commit to avoiding those mistakes. Simple, right?

Unfortunately, that's just not the way it works. The best way young people learn is the same way we did: through personal experience. But we don't want to wait until they battle insecurities and have to choose between doing the wrong thing to gain popularity or doing the righteous thing and facing ridicule. So, other than the obvious, what else can we do? This is where these Hot Buttons books come in. When we use the Strategic Scenarios, purposeful dialogue about hot-button issues will provide us the opportunity to sneak in something resembling personal experience for our kids—without the dreaded ramifications—while also teaching them that their opinions, thoughts, and feelings are important and valid.

Combat the lies with the truth.

We know Satan's plan:

> He was a murderer from the beginning, not holding to the truth, for **there is no truth in him**. When he lies, he speaks his native language, for **he is a liar and the father of lies**. (John 8:44)

Satan wants to trap teens into making a huge mistake by trading a satisfying self-image for insecurity and self-doubt. As we've already covered earlier in this book, we know our battle is ultimately fought on the spiritual level as we ward off his fiery darts. Those arrows from the enemy often come in the form of lies.

Here are some of the biggies related to image:

Lie #1: If you give in this time, they'll be your friends.
> *Truth:* The peer pressure never ends. The boundary line will likely continue to move to keep the friends.

Lie #2: If you have sex with him (her), he'll (she'll) love you.
> *Truth:* Most teen sexual relationships end fewer than six months later and twenty-five percent of them are one-time events and actually end the relationship.

Lie #3: If you lose weight, they'll let you in their group.
> *Truth:* You don't want friends who hold weight as a condition for friendship. Lose weight to live a healthy life.

Proactive: Answering *How*

Lie #4: If you look like _____ (insert celebrity), you'll be popular.

> *Truth:* _____ (insert celebrity) doesn't even look like that, thanks to makeup artists, stylists, and airbrushing.

Your beauty should not come from outward adornment, such as elaborate hairstyles and the wearing of gold jewelry or fine clothes. Rather, **it should be that of your inner self**, the unfading beauty of a gentle and quiet spirit, **which is of great worth in God's sight**. (1 Peter 3:3–4)

But the LORD said to Samuel, "Do not consider his appearance or his height, for I have rejected him. **The LORD does not look at the things people look at**. People look at the outward appearance, but **the LORD looks at the heart**." (1 Sam. 16:7)

Where do we go from here?

Hot Buttons Image Edition is a manual for those important, preemptive and ongoing discussions you need to have with your tweens and teens about self-esteem, body image, celebrity, popularity, and other things that go along with that topic. Here in part 1, we've covered the whys and hows of confronting the issue preemptively and what to watch out for along the way. Part 2 looks at the specifics of the image pressures your teens and preteens face these days.

In part 3, we'll actually do it. You'll be able to take away practical and precise words in the form of Strategic Scenarios that will help you press the hot buttons that relate to image and popularity. Issues like peer pressure, eating disorders, popularity, modesty, dating, and friendships will each have several scenarios for you to work through with your teen. I'll share truths about the topic, help you figure out how to handle it in your own home, and offer a prayer you can pray to ask God to help you with that certain issue.

Let's stop being horrified by the truth about what our teens are faced with and start doing something to equip them to handle it. This book deals with self-esteem, body image, celebrity influences, and the various dangers that accompany those things. When you turn up the heat on this issue, you might see smoke in every direction that signals there's already a fire smoldering somewhere in your home. It's okay—but it's time to get serious. Remember: God is in control.

CHECK POINTS ▶▶▶

CHECK POINTS

✓ Studies have shown that teens feel the most distance from parents who try to be their friends. They have peers at school. At home, they need and want a parent.

✓ Parents, you're going to want to set firm boundaries about the clothing choices your teens make, so it's necessary that you're a good role model. Your teens don't want you to dress like them—they just want you to blend in with the other parents.

✓ Praise inner beauty over outer—and not just when it's your only choice.

✓ When asked what teens don't like about adults, the biggest complaint is that parents don't really take the time to listen. If parents aren't listening, and kids feel alone, of course they're going to look elsewhere for guidance—the media, their friends, and celebrities.

✓ If you pretend you were someone you weren't, you might tip the scales in the wrong direction as your teen is unable to relate to you and your supposed choices. It helps when teenagers can see their parents as human beings with weaknesses, failures, and struggles. They don't feel so alone in the battle.

✓ Young people learn best through personal experience, but we don't want to wait until they battle insecurities and have to choose between doing the wrong thing to gain popularity or doing the righteous thing and facing ridicule.

PART TWO

Identifying the Image HOT BUTTONS

What do the hot buttons of self-image look like?

Are they the same for every person?

Will I know them when I see them?

Those are all questions we must ask. And it's important that we get answers so we can move forward in preparing our tweens for what lies ahead. As I showed in the previous chapters, the answers to those questions and the preparation done in response to them could have saved me from an out-of-control downward spiral.

It's natural for Christian parents to have an unspoken expectation that their kids are immune to some of the worldly pitfalls that exist—even the ones parents themselves succumbed to when they were teens. I catch myself assuming that my kids inherently "get it" on certain things, and then I wonder why I would dare assume such a thing. They aren't born with a perfect understanding of right and wrong, nor with the resolve to always do the right thing. That has to be taught. They certainly aren't born with godly perspective about their individual worth and beauty. That has to be learned and reinforced over time.

Hopefully these next few chapters will enlighten you to the risks your teens face and help you prepare them for the tough choices ahead.

Popularity

On the issue of self-image, I thought it prudent to begin by briefly touching on the topic of popularity. It weaves itself in and throughout the other segments of this book, and it's covered in great detail in *Hot Buttons Bullying Edition*. It needs inclusion here as well, though, since much of our teenagers' image struggles are either rooted in or lead to the popularity battle.

In Pursuit of Popularity

When teens have a healthy self-image, they may have many friends and be popular because it's easy to like those who generally like themselves. But teens with an unhealthy self-image often chase popularity in an effort to find identity and validation.

It's often the pursuit of popularity that causes someone to submit to bullying, or it's the desperation to hold on to a social status that leads to bullying others. And that same desire can lead teenagers to make bad choices in response to peer pressure in hopes of winning the favor of someone whom they perceive as cooler or more popular. In all of those examples, it's a self-image problem that drives the behavior.

When that boy, the one who had bullied me mercilessly, paid positive attention to me on the first day of high school, I subconsciously put structure to all I believed about myself and about what it took to get by in the world. I adopted the belief that popularity was all that mattered and appearance was the best way to attain it. And if I wanted to get the attention of boys or anyone, I'd better capitalize on my looks whenever I could.

So I did.

In the months following that incident, I had increasing opportunity to skyrocket my social status and I did whatever it took. I wasn't going to allow myself to ever again feel like I'd felt during middle school, which was my fault after all. Wasn't it?

"If I hadn't gained all that weight . . ."

"If I'd been cooler . . ."

"If I'd fit into trendy clothes . . ."

"If I'd been able to participate in sports . . ."

You see, when I was able to dress in the perfect clothes, when I did well on the swim team, when I got my hair cut the way the popular girls wore theirs, when I said yes to peer pressure, when I alienated my old friends, I was popular. It worked!

But there was a huge cost that I hadn't considered at the time.

The choices I made in pursuit of popularity cost me the respect and trust of my parents. I lost the BFF I'd had since first grade—one of the few who'd stuck by me through the tough middle school years—because she

Popularity

wasn't "cool" enough and we no longer had anything in common. And it didn't take very long at all for my grades to fall along with my self-respect.

Eventually, it cost me my virginity as I was date-raped, and then I followed that with one bad choice after another looking for that elusive acceptance that would finally stick.

Popularity Versus Likeability

Often kids who are thought to be popular—you know, the ones at the top of the heap, the ones who call the shots—aren't always well liked. They hold their status as a means of control, and others cater to them out of fear, not out of a genuine desire to have a friendship with that person. In that way, seeking a relationship with those types becomes more of a means to an end than an effort at a true friendship.

Being popular, in the sense of what most of our kids think popularity is, does not equate to happiness or fulfillment. In fact, it's often rooted in fear. Fear of losing hold of that status. Fear of messing up. Fear of being found inadequate or fake. Popular people are under all sorts of pressure to keep that popularity. That kind of pressure can lead to depression, unhappiness, and bad choices as they struggle to keep that which they've worked so hard to attain.

But likeability is something different. Likeability is attained because of a person's true identity. It's not earned or even sought. It's the result of truth. When a teenager is true to what's actually inside and still manages to have good friends, that is so validating. But when someone must be fake in order to have friendships, confidence and self-value are stripped.

So, if not popularity, what?

If we aren't to encourage our teens to chase after popularity, how do we steer them toward a life rich with relationships and fulfillment? After all, having friends is important. Isn't it?

Of course it is.

We definitely don't want to pull them so far back that they are alone or cast out of having a good middle school or high school experience. Somewhere in the middle is where the healthy place exists.

We want to encourage our tweens and teens to find their own way to leading a fulfilling life and to having good, godly friends. This is an intentional choice and it goes against what society preaches and what the bullies might want. Because, in that place, our kids are untouchable. If they have no desire to fight for position or approval, then peer pressure loses its sting.

To help your tweens and teens be intentional about shaping a healthy existence for themselves, there are some things you can do:

> ➤ *Encourage them to join clubs or teams that feed their personal interests.* There's probably no better way to find kids who share common goals and enjoy the same things. Help them feed the special talents and interests God gave them.
> ➤ *Help your kids take pride in their appearance.* This is different than buying all the trendy clothes or dressing to gain approval. This is about hygiene and a general sense of health and taking care of themselves.
> ➤ *Encourage them to make good choices.* Staying true to their values will set them apart and make them appealing to other kids who

are doing the same. These Hot Buttons books are helping you guide them to good choices.

> *Build their confidence.* Encourage your tweens and teens with positive feedback. Compliment them publicly and draw them out in conversations. Self-confidence is a very attractive quality. This also translates into the ability to stand up against peer pressure and bullying.

> *Teach them to be kind.* Likeable people are genuinely kind to others. Teach them to share compliments, offer a kind word, be available to help or counsel others, and generally think of others first. Kind people are not exclusionary in their friendships.

Those are just a few good places to start as you work on raising well-adjusted tweens and teens with a positive, healthy self-image. We'll continue to revisit the popularity issue throughout this book as it naturally weaves itself into much of the discussion of self-image. I'd also encourage you to pick up *Hot Buttons Bullying Edition* as it dives even deeper into the behaviors and thought patterns that drive teens to seek popularity at any cost.

Popularity is a state of mind, and it's up to each individual to decide not to grant that kind of power to others, whether as a result of intentional peer pressure and bullying or not. Why let someone else decide one's worth? Why submit to someone else's arbitrary standards? When our tweens and teens are able to ask themselves those questions, and when they are able to see themselves the way God does and reject the cost that comes with the chase for popularity in favor of building their self-worth and remaining true to themselves, they will find fulfillment.

Lord, please help me instill a positive self-image in my kids. Let them catch a glimpse of who they are in Your eyes so they can love themselves a little more each day. Help them avoid the trappings of the popularity battle, and guide them to those few good friends who will be a healthy influence in their lives. Protect them from peer pressure, and help me to see areas of concern so I can address them right away. Thank You for guiding me as I parent them. Amen.

CHECK POINTS ➤➤➤

CHECK POINTS

✓ When teens have a healthy self-image, they may have many friends and be popular because it's easy to like those who generally like themselves. But teens with an unhealthy self-image often chase popularity in an effort to find identity and validation.

✓ It's often the pursuit of popularity that causes someone to submit to bullying, or it's the desperation to hold on to a social status that leads to bullying others. And that same desire often leads teenagers to make bad choices in response to peer pressure in hopes of winning the favor of someone whom they perceive as cooler or more popular. In all of those examples, it's a self-image problem that drives the behavior.

✓ Often kids who are thought to be popular . . . aren't always well liked. They hold their status as a means of control, and others cater to them out of fear, not out of a genuine desire to have a friendship with that person.

✓ Likeability is attained because of a person's true identity. It's not earned or even sought. It's the result of truth.

✓ If your kids have no desire to fight for position or approval, then peer pressure loses its sting.

✓ When people are able to see themselves the way God does and reject the cost that comes with the chase for popularity in favor of building their self-worth and remaining true to themselves, they will find fulfillment.

Self-Esteem

I have often wondered how it is everyone loves himself more than the rest of men, but yet sets less value on his own opinions of himself than the opinions of others.

—MARCUS AURELIUS

Self-esteem is simply how you feel about yourself and how confident you are in your own success. For example, people with high self-esteem focus on personal growth and improvement in various areas of life, whereas people with low self-esteem focus on not making mistakes or disappointing others.[1] According to researchers, people with low self-esteem are more troubled by failure and tend to exaggerate events as being negative. They tend to misread comments and assume people are being critical of or judgmental toward them. This makes social interaction awkward, as they are unable to adequately express themselves.[2]

Girls with low self-esteem tend to struggle with body image issues, eating disorders, celebrity obsessions, and more. (Later chapters in this book will cover all of those.) Other issues related to low self-esteem can affect boys and girls equally, though sometimes in different ways:

- Dating violence
- Premarital sex
- Drug and alcohol abuse
- Teen pregnancy
- Being bullied and bullying
- Tattoos
- Excessive piercings and other forms of body modifications
- Gang association or membership
- Self-harm
- Suicide

Internal and External Sources

Self-esteem can be further dissembled into two categories: self-esteem rooted in external sources, and self-esteem based on internal sources.

External sources include accomplishments, successes, and visible achievements. External self-esteem is based on popularity or whatever motivates an individual based on the perceptions or opinions of other people or outside influences. It's dangerous because it's fleeting. What if your teenager is top of the heap at youth group, but bullied and un-popular at school? That's an extreme example, but it shows the possible confusion that can happen when external reasons for self-esteem come and go. This type is fleeting and not rooted in the "person" but rather in extraneous things that can't often be forced, which leads to endless striving for that elusive approval.

Internal sources of self-esteem are what parents want to focus on. The source of healthy self-esteem is internal, in response to God's Word. It's what a person takes along from place to place; it's believing the truth about oneself and others. It doesn't have anything to do with outside success, but rather it's based on the intrinsic value a person finds within. Studies have found that "students who based their self-esteem on internal sources—such as being a virtuous person or adhering to moral standards—were found to receive higher grades and less likely to use alcohol and drugs or to develop eating disorders" than those who based their self-esteem on external sources, such as academic performance![3]

Often, an unhealthy self-esteem comes from looking to externals to fix the internal.

"If I lose weight, I'll be happy."

"If I have a nose job, I'll feel loved."

"If I drive a new car, I'll feel successful."

"If I date the most popular girl, I'll feel accepted."

Looking to a temporary, external thing as the means to permanently repair internal damage is like paying the mortgage with a credit card—the fix is temporary, and the cost is astronomical, compounding whatever problems already exist. In the lives of teenagers, for whom everything changes on a weekly or daily basis, those temporary fixes will come at great cost. Can you imagine the mental and emotional roller-coaster ride that would cause? Says, Jennifer Crocker, a psychologist at the University of Michigan's Institute for Social Research, students who look to the external of success in academics, for instance, may do well, "but having their self-worth on the line doesn't help their performance." Instead, they may "become anxious and distracted and threatened by feelings of failure."[4]

The Choice

So much of this issue comes back to choice. In my case, I had a choice in how I would let the initial physical changes affect my perception of my self-worth—whether or not others agreed. I had a choice whether or not to give power to the bullies or voice to the "populars." Then I had a choice as to whether or not I'd give in to the pressures when popularity was within reach. But my filter was faulty. I allowed the lies of the enemy and the voices of others to sift through the filter of low self-esteem, as so many teenagers do.

The Filter of Self-Esteem

Everything you take in—thoughts, beliefs, words people say, and compliments from others—runs through a filter of healthy or low self-esteem. If you're able to objectively look at the way your teenager processes those things I mentioned, it'll help you identify the self-esteem condition at work.

> **Compliment:** "Wow, that color looks amazing on you."
> **Low self-esteem filter:** Which means I look horrible in everything else.
> **Healthy self-esteem filter:** It's because it complements my eye color.

Thought: Cheerleaders have the coolest friends.
Low self-esteem filter: They'll never let me into their group.
Healthy self-esteem filter: If they knew me, they'd love me—their loss.

Belief: Only graduates from Ivy League universities get good jobs.
Low self-esteem filter: I'll never get in, so there's no point in trying.
Healthy self-esteem filter: I'll apply myself to studying diligently, and
see if my grades are high enough for admittance. What's the worst
that can happen? My grades will be better.

Desire: "I love you, baby. I want to be with you forever."
Low self-esteem filter: I should have sex with him so he'll stay with me.
Healthy self-esteem filter: I am worth waiting for.

Promise: "I'm sorry I hit you. I'll never, ever do it again."
Low self-esteem filter: I probably deserved it, and he promises . . .
Healthy self-esteem filter: I deserve better, and he deserves conse-
quences for his actions.

Markers of Healthy Self-Esteem

Instead of focusing on how not to look at life and self, let's examine what it
looks like to have a healthy self-esteem. Along with the other recommendations in this book, consider talking with your teens about the following
ten markers that describe the way people with a healthy self-esteem look
at themselves and at life. You might be surprised at how illuminating it is.

Ten markers of healthy self-esteem:

1. *Has a general sense of being worthy of the love and approval of others.*
   He's not shocked that someone might find value in him; in fact, he expects it, because he believes what God says about him.

2. *Is committed to strongly defined values.*
   She knows what she believes and why. She's not tempted to abandon her faith in pursuit of popularity or the approval of others. She doesn't have trouble standing against peer pressure.

3. *Knows strengths and capitalizes on them, and uses weaknesses as areas for growth.*
   He's under no delusions about his own perfection, but he does know he has certain God-given talents and abilities and is happy to contribute when he can. Weak areas aren't failures; they're just places where growth can happen.

4. *Listens to constructive criticism and measures it carefully.*
   She welcomes constructive criticism and sees it as an opportunity, not a personal affront. When someone offers a criticism, she considers its merit and applies it for change when appropriate or tucks it aside for later when it's not.

5. *Feels confident in being able to solve any challenges that come.*
   He rarely crumbles under pressure. He looks for the solution to any problem or challenge, because he's confident it's there.

6. *Exudes openness and acceptance of others.*
   People don't shy away from her. They know she's a friend and they don't hesitate to approach in friendship or for counsel. People often say she's everyone's BFF, meaning they feel no exclusivity coming from her.

7. *Has a thought-out opinion, is willing to share it, and isn't afraid of disagreement.*

   He is able to consider both sides of an argument and formulate his own opinion. He's able to share thoughts with others whether they agree with him or not. He's not arrogant in his position but loving in his explanation.

8. *Laughs.*

   Joy comes from within and she's bubbling over with it. God has given her a merry heart and she's not afraid to share it with others.

9. *Knows self: goals, desires, dreams.*

   He knows what he wants out of life—short term or long term—and isn't afraid to chase hard after it. He expects to achieve his goals because he believes in himself and in God's power.

10. *Believes the sky is the limit for growth potential.*

    She believes that God has started a great work in her, but is so happy to know that the work isn't finished yet. She believe His promise that He's going to continue to perfect His work and His plans in her until the day she stands before Jesus (Phil. 1:6).

Ultimately, the goal is to have a healthy, godly self-esteem.

Need More Convincing?

Nick Vujicic was born without arms or legs. He had a rough childhood full of humiliation and bullying of all kinds. He felt utterly worthless, hopeless about his future, and like a complete burden to his parents. At the age of ten, Nick attempted to drown himself.

In an episode of *Oprah's Lifeclass* with Rick Warren, Nick said, "Parents,

I want you to know something very, very important. If it wasn't for my parents, my heroes, who planted those seeds of love and truth and hope in my life, I wouldn't be here today." He looked at the teary audience. "When your teenager hears you say 'You're beautiful' then hangs a 'Do not Disturb' sign on their door, I want you to respect that, but go through their window."[5]

You see, our enemy assures us the next thing will make us happy. Losing weight will solve our problems. If only we didn't have _____ cross to bear, then we'd be popular. . . . If we found a boyfriend, got a better wardrobe, had our hair restyled. Those lies and others like them are pelting your teenagers on a moment-by-moment basis. But they're looking for the wrong things in the wrong places. They need you to guide their eyes upward.

It's all there. All the hope, love, peace, joy, and fulfillment they could ever want from life. At the feet of Jesus. That's the source of a healthy, internally motivated self-image. One moment of feeling His embrace and unconditional love, one pure glimpse of the truth of His plans, and the rest will fade away.

It's not an easy battle and when won, it doesn't stay won without constant gut checks and reminders. But once the source has been found, it never disappears.

What does God say about perfectionism?

It's a good thing when your teenager wants to give the very best to anything. We're told in God's Word that we should do everything as though we're doing it for Him (Col. 3:23), for His glory (1 Cor. 10:31). High standards are good, even important for the believer. But when we set our sights on being *perfect*, that becomes about us, not Him.

We need to remind our teenagers that God came for us. He chased us down. He made the first move in a broad, life-changing, love-pouring event in which He proved His acceptance of us even when we were still sinners.

> But God demonstrates his own love for us in this: **While we were still sinners, Christ died for us**. (Rom. 5:8)

Being perfect in Christ means being perfectly sanctified, washed in His blood, free from the darkness of sin. Really, in light of that, how can we consume ourselves with temporary things?

Yes, you might get an eye roll when you express that to your kids. I remember thinking that God was separate from my day-to-day life. I knew He was awesome, and I was so glad to have Him in my life. But I didn't think He could do much for me at school, so I had to do what I had to do just to get by. It really shows a misunderstanding about God, and, if we're being honest, a lack of relationship with Him. So, if you see those signs, that's where you should put your first efforts. Let your teenager really meet Jesus. The self-esteem will follow.

Lord, the issues of self-esteem are far-reaching and the thought of all the doubts and pressures that assault my teens brings me to my knees. Please grant me Your wisdom to see destructive thoughts and patterns before they become a problem. Help me know what to do to keep my teens on a path toward a healthy, godly self-esteem. Let them flee the lie of worthlessness and run just as hard from the arrogance of self-importance. Let my teens rest securely in your arms. Confident. Valued. Loved. Amen.

CHECK POINTS

✓ People with high self-esteem focus on personal growth and improvement in various areas of life, whereas people with low self-esteem focus on not making mistakes or disappointing others.

✓ The source of healthy self-esteem is internal, in response to God's Word. It's what a person takes along from place to place; it's believing the truth about oneself and others.

✓ Everything you take in—thoughts, beliefs, words people say, and compliments from others—runs through a filter of healthy or low self-esteem.

✓ "When your teenager hears you say 'You're beautiful' then hangs a 'Do not Disturb' sign on their door, I want you to respect that, but go through their window."[6]

✓ You see, our enemy assures us the next thing will make us happy. Those lies and others like them are pelting your teenagers on a moment-by-moment basis. But they're looking for the wrong things in the wrong places. They need you to turn their eyes upward.

✓ It's all there. All the hope, love, peace, joy, and fulfillment they could ever want from life. At the feet of Jesus. That's the source of healthy internal self-image. One moment of feeling His embrace and unconditional love, one pure glimpse of the truth of His plans, and the rest will fade away.

Body Image

Body image is how a person views their physical self. That includes not only height and weight but every aspect of every feature on one's body. How often have you heard someone complain about the shape of their toes or chin? The curl—or lack thereof—of their hair; the imperfections on their fingernails; the protrusion of their belly button? No body part is exempt from scrutiny. From chest to hips to knees, both males and females stress over perceived inadequacies.

The Truth About Self-Perception

According to the website of a teen treatment center, 53 percent of American girls say they're unhappy with their bodies at age thirteen. That number grows to 78 percent by age seventeen.[7]

You can imagine how body image affected my choices and the way I saw myself. I had no concept of the truth about my body. Have you ever gone to an event looking pretty great? New slinky dress from a high-end store. Great shoes. Perfect makeup. Everything was just right—the only thing missing was the red carpet.

Then, weeks later (or hours if some snappy Facebooker gets inspired) you see a picture of yourself. You're horrified to see the dress looks awful from the back or that your new hair color actually has a greenish glow under the flash of a camera. And the muffin top? Where did that come from?

That's how I felt most of the time.

I either had no idea what size I was, or I thought I looked better than I actually did. Disparities on both extremes. I remember shopping with my mom one time. I held up this really cute brown shirt. She loved it, but recommended I get it in my size.

"What? It's an XL. That should fit me okay. Even better when I lose a few more pounds."

Mom scoffed. "That's going to be way too big for you, Nicole."

I held it up and peered at it more closely. Could she be right? I reached for a large and slipped my arms in the sleeves. It was too big. A medium? I couldn't wear a medium! That's what the small, pretty girls wore. Not me.

On top of the misperceptions caused by self-doubt, tweens and teens are in a constant state of flux. Their bodies are changing rapidly, and sometimes they're hyperaware of every little change, while other times they need time to catch their brains up to their bodies. Then there's the celebrity image perpetuated by the media that sets a bar too high for any human being to attain—even the celebs themselves. We'll go into more detail in chapter 7 about the influence of celebrities and the media.

Boys Struggle Too

Though the statistics show that girls suffer under the weight of body image concerns more than boys do, many teenage boys do compare themselves to others and feel dissatisfied if they don't measure up. Height, weight, skin condition, hair, and other aspects of appearance can have a harsh effect on boys as well as girls.

Bullying and insecurities seem to affect boys who are overweight and underweight equally even though they aren't usually as open about their body image struggles as girls are. Many face depression or eating disorders, and undertake other risky and destructive behaviors, like getting tattoos and piercings, as a result.

The current trend for teenage boys is toward a beefy, muscular physique. In a study published in the journal *Pediatrics*, 40 percent of boys in middle and high school say they regularly exercise to increase muscle mass; 38 percent take protein supplements for the same reason; and almost 6 percent admit to experimenting with illegal steroids.[8]

They're chasing the magazine covers just like the girls are, but what they are missing, just like the girls, is that virtually none of those images are of high-school-aged boys and all of them are airbrushed. They're chasing an ideal that doesn't exist and competing against images that aren't even real.

What can YOU do?

Awareness is the most important tool in dealing with the issues related to body-image struggles. Knowing in advance the types of problems your teens could face puts you at a huge advantage as you prepare to deal with them. Know signs of body-image battles so you can address them at the earliest possible stage.

Signs of body-image disturbance in your teen can include:

- ➤ Obsessed with appearance
- ➤ Picks on a certain body part: nose, eyes, hips . . .
- ➤ Constantly looks in mirrors
- ➤ Avoids mirrors
- ➤ Talks about appearance excessively
- ➤ Avoids having picture taken
- ➤ Compares self to others
- ➤ Avoids socializing when it means dressing up
- ➤ Camouflages, like with excessive makeup or layers of clothing

Also, your own lifestyle and words are powerful in either helping or harming your child's body-image. Your tweens and teens, boys and girls, are watching you. They notice things like what, when, and how much you eat. They pay attention to your attitudes about your own body and internalize your comments about weight and dieting. The way you see yourself is the way your kids will see themselves. If you're always picking on yourself, your child will do the same.

You might start to notice times you're able to change the way you say something, or even if you say it at all. Let your kids' needs be a motivator for adopting healthy attitudes and lifestyles to benefit the entire family.

Never make critical remarks about your teenager's weight or body type. In fact, try to focus your compliments on internal traits like kindness, generosity, and other Christlike qualities. Compliments about the physical are nice, but for both girls and boys, they mainly serve to keep the focus on appearance.

Try to reinforce behaviors and traits that have eternal value. "You're such a good big brother, I know little Johnny appreciates it when you give him time." Or, "You're a great example for the younger girls in church. Keep making good choices." And when you do compliment the physical, keep the comparisons at bay by drawing the attention inward with comment like, "Your eyes look especially pretty when you smile."

Encourage the development of interests that have nothing to do with appearance. Being involved in a team sport, playing in the school band, nurturing a passion for art, whatever it is, is a great way to nurture qualities other than those based on appearance. This advice is especially pertinent when you have kids who possess different amounts of the *pretty* gene. The other sibling is at risk for appearance-based anxiety unless you create an environment in which other traits, skills, and characteristics are more valued.

Good Talk Versus Trash Talk

How we portray our outlook on our own health, fitness, body image, diets, and lifestyle choices to our families has a profound effect on how they view themselves. What do you think happens when our girls watch our back-and-forth dilemma over every bite we eat? They begin to speak judgment on themselves and fall into dieting extremes. What do you think they feel when we don't want to go out on Friday night because we have nothing to wear? They trash their own value with the perception that they aren't worth your effort. How do you think they feel about us when we can never relax and enjoy a nice meal including dessert? They belittle their own perceived lack of self-control. And how do you think they feel about themselves when we refuse to put our insecurities aside to spend a day at the beach or a water park with them? They come to believe they're less important than how you think you look.

So, with all that internal trash talk, how will they feel about themselves at our age?

And how will their children, our grandchildren, feel about watching the cycle repeat itself?

Because it will.

In order to break the cycle of trash talk, we need to be intentional about speaking life into our children. They will learn that we love ourselves and them; or they will learn that we're unsatisfied and unsuccessful . . . and ungrateful. So here's my list of ten things you shouldn't say, and what you should say instead.

> **Don't say:** I'm too fat. I wish there were a pill I could take to make it all go away.
>
> **Do say:** I'd love to trim up a bit so I can be more active. I'm researching healthy ways to do that. Want to help me?

> **Don't say:** I can't eat that. A moment on the lips, a lifetime on the hips.
>
> **Do say:** A whole serving might not be the healthiest choice for me right now, but I'd love to taste yours.

> **Don't say:** Sorry, can't hang out right now—I need to spend two hours on the treadmill.
>
> **Do say:** I'd love to hang out, but I had planned to exercise. How about a nice, long walk together?

Don't say: She's so tall and gorgeous! Must be good genes.

Do say: *Nothing.* (There's no need to make comparisons or draw attention to someone else's looks. In commenting on one person's looks, you are automatically judging—by omission—someone else's, and your kids will take note if they don't measure up.)

Don't say: You sure you want to eat that? I was skinny like you once, too.

Do say: For health reasons, you might want to check the serving size.

Don't say: Yes, I'm going to wear these ten-year-old sweatpants to your school. Why bother dressing up? It's not going to help.

Do say: Give me a second to put on something appropriate.

Don't say: No way am I going to my high school reunion. Next to all those tan, highlighted, manicured women who have time for the gym every day . . . I'll look frumpy!

Do say: Of course I'm going to go. How else could I show everyone pictures and brag on my kids?

Don't say: Sure. We'll take a beach vacation after I lose twenty pounds.

Do say: We're going to the beach with no electronics—a day just for us!

Don't say: Sorry sweetie, genes are cruel. You're destined to have hips just like mine.

Do say: I think it's great you're focused on health and fitness already. You're destined to have a healthy, active life.

Don't say: If only . . .
Do say: I'm so grateful to God for my health and beauty . . . and for you!

Recommendations

As with everything, Mom and Dad, moderation is key. Consider how the following specific lifestyle choices might help your family rise to a new level of mental, physical, and spiritual health.

- Limit things like fast food, junk food, and processed meals.
- Ramp up the use of fresh veggies, fruits, lean meats.
- Pull out recipe books and take joy in trying new things.
- Get active together by going on walks, bike rides, etc.
- Talk about health and fitness as positives, not negatives.
- Have regular family meals at a set time.
- Limit or eliminate after-dinner snacking.
- Limit or eliminate soft drinks in favor of water.
- Practice good talk rather than trash talk.
- Get medical help or counseling when it's necessary.

Plan to start small and work together to make these changes. One suggestion that might help is something I've done with my girls. I assigned them one night a week to plan dinner. They could pick any recipe from a cookbook and were responsible for making sure the ingredients were all available. They cooked it and served it, giving them great insight into what goes into meal planning and providing for a family in a healthy way.

Don't try to do everything at once. That's the fast track to burnout and failure. Just pray about the areas where God would have you begin to make small changes. Let Him show you where He wants your focus to be at any given time. The biggest thing is to work on getting yourself mentally and physically healthy so you can be an example of moderation and so you can show what it really means to place value on yourself.

Father, it breaks my heart to think that my kids don't see the beauty that I see when I look at them. Please help me to have a positive effect on their self-esteem and to give them good feedback and inspiration when it comes to their bodies. Help me guide my teens to have a long-term perspective on health and good living rather than a short-term view that seeks the approval of others and leads to crash diets and eating disorders. Show me what I need to see, and give me the right questions to ask so I can uncover their insecurities and deal with them. Thank You for loving them. Amen.

CHECK POINTS ▶▶▶

CHECK POINTS

✓ On top of the misperceptions caused by self-doubt, tweens and teens are in a constant state of flux. Their bodies are changing rapidly, and sometimes they're hyperaware of every little change, while other times they need time to catch their brains up to their bodies.

✓ Your tweens and teens, boys and girls, are watching you. They notice things like what, when, and how much you eat. They pay attention to your attitudes about your own body and internalize your comments about weight and dieting. The way you see yourself is the way your kids will see themselves.

✓ Encourage the development of interests that have nothing to do with appearance.

✓ In order to break the cycle of trash talk, we need to be intentional about speaking life into our children. They will learn that we love ourselves and them; or they will learn that we're unsatisfied and unsuccessful . . . and ungrateful.

✓ As with everything, Mom and Dad, moderation is key. Consider how some specific lifestyle choices might help your family rise to a new level of mental, physical, and spiritual health.

✓ Plan to start small and work together to make changes.

Eating Disorders

As a teenager, I desperately wished I could be anorexic.

I don't know that I've ever admitted that before now. But, truly, I thought the skinny, anorexic girls were the strong ones. They were masters over food and they reaped the rewards. They fit into clothes I could never dream of wearing—at least at that time. They were the lucky ones people begged with comments like:

> **"Please eat something!"**
> **"Here, have some cake."**
> **"Oh, aren't your going to finish your fries?"**

No one ever worried about me finishing my fries. I think, for me, the roller coaster of having the encephalitis, gaining all that weight, suffering the attacks of bullies, then losing the weight, being hit on by the bullies . . . I was just so messed up in my thinking. I didn't know if I was fat or thin, ugly or pretty, healthy or unhealthy. And I didn't care.

I just wanted to be the skinny, popular girl people had to force-feed.

My entire life became a game of yo-yo dieting. I got really good at it, too. I tried them all and they all worked for a time. With each baby I packed on more and more weight and dealt with more and more food sensitivities that cropped up with each pregnancy and never left. One time I had a chiropractor do a really expensive food allergy test and it turned out I was allergic to most things high in carbohydrates. So, I went on the Atkins diet and lost over 100 pounds.

I was working out like crazy—Biggest Loser style—and then I got a job at a gym and exercised and weight trained even more. I really love exercise and the more extreme, the better. Then it happened . . . one day my husband said, "Um, I think you're losing too much weight; I can see your ribs." He said it hesitantly because he thought it was an insult.

Silly man! It actually excited me so much that it spurred me on to more weight loss.

Then I got pregnant with the triplets. How sad is it that my very first thought upon seeing three heartbeats on that ultrasound screen was that I would gain weight? Can you imagine the panic I felt when the doctor said I'd need to gain close to 100 pounds to give them the healthiest start possible?

So I did . . . and they were born healthy . . . and I'm still fighting to take that weight off.

Why am I telling you this? Mainly to show that we all have a story. We all have our body struggles, and what goes on in one person's head might be different than what another person is thinking, but it's all rooted in the same place of dissatisfaction.

I don't have a formal eating disorder like anorexia or bulimia, but I have definitely spent most of my life dealing with disordered eating, a poor body image, and yo-yo dieting.

What are eating disorders?

The most common eating disorders are anorexia and bulimia. There are many other ways to participate in what I'll call disordered eating like binge eating, food phobias, use of laxatives or diet pills, yo-yo dieting, and more. Around 15 percent of teenage girls have some type of eating disorder or disordered-eating behavior.[9]

Anorexia

People with anorexia have true anxiety at the thought of weight gain. Many times they can't see the truth about their body so they don't know when to quit. Anorexia for both teenagers and adults involves food restriction by dieting, fasting, or excessive exercise—or, commonly, some combination of the three. Anorexics hardly eat anything, and each bite becomes an obsession or is surrounded by dread. An estimated 5 percent of adolescent girls are currently suffering from anorexia.[10]

Teens with anorexia are usually terrified of being overweight. They spend an inordinate amount of time looking in the mirror, pinching nonexistent fat, or thinking they're obese when they are actually thin. Anorexics often weigh food or count calories over and over. To them, this is normal behavior and they get irritated or agitated if anyone suggests otherwise, wishing people would just mind their own business. Because of the pressure they feel from others, they try to avoid situations when their birdlike portions would be obvious. It doesn't take long for this behavior to lead to malnourishment, dehydration, fainting or dizzy spells, mood swings, and other health complications.

The specific cause of anorexia is unknown, but it's clearly tied to body image issues and self-esteem problems. Insecurity leads to excessive goals—usually unnecessary and unattainable—in order to achieve an ideal. They will never be satisfied. Anorexia is like trying to fill a strainer with water.

Some side effects of anorexia include:

- Low blood pressure
- Hair loss
- Stopped or delayed menstruation
- Fine hair growing all over the skin
- Lightheadedness, dizziness
- Fainting
- Weakness
- Muscle loss
- Vitamin deficiency

Bulimia

Bulimia is similar to anorexia in that those who suffer with it struggle with self-control and an inaccurate perception of their own bodies, but in the case of bulimia, self-loathing drives sufferers to induce vomiting after eating. One difference is that bulimics are not usually underweight. They are often an average weight or even overweight. One reason for that is many bulimics binge eat and then purge. This means that they consume a lot of food (often junk food, and often secretly) and then attempt to rid themselves of the calories by vomiting or using laxatives.

Bulimics feel so powerless to control their compulsion that they might scarf down uncooked or even frozen food, or eat food out of the trash. I knew of one bulimic who used to try to stop herself from eating poorly. She'd take whatever junk food item she was tempted to consume, throw it in the garbage, and pour soggy coffee grounds on top of it. The sad thing is she retrieved that food item, wiped it off, and ate it. More than once.

Bulimics typically feel powerless to stop the eating and can only stop once they're too full to eat any more. Most people with bulimia then purge by vomiting, but may also use laxatives or exercise excessively.

Watch for signs of major dietary changes, heading to the bathroom immediately after eating, excessive exercise or food restrictions, and bingeing. Also, watch for evidence of laxatives, diuretics, or enemas. If you find such empty packaging in the trash, for example, it's something to address—a teenager should not be using those products for any reason without medical supervision.

Side effects specific to bulimia because of the constant vomiting and lack of nutrients include:

- Stomach pain, cramps
- Organ damage
- Tooth decay and enamel problems due to exposure to stomach acids
- Puffy cheeks due to expanded salivary glands
- Stopped or delayed menstruation
- Potassium deficiency

Eating Disorders

Bingeing

This is similar to bulimia because a person binges a few times a week or more, but differs because it doesn't involve inducing vomiting to purge the food. Not to be confused with normal, albeit uncomfortable, overeating that occurs once in a while due to things like celebrations or holidays, binge disorder leads to compulsive overeating on a regular basis.

Since bingeing leads to the consumption of way more calories than the average person can burn, bingers are usually overweight or obese. This leads to less and less activity, depression, regret, stress, and other emotional disturbances that naturally lead to more overeating and more weight gain. It's a vicious cycle of comfort eating, weight gain, depression, comfort eating, weight gain . . .

Symptoms include:

- Lack of control over type or amount of food consumed
- Eats quickly
- Hides food and eats in secret
- Eats even when stuffed
- Uses food as comfort
- Rarely seems satisfied
- Desperate to lose weight

Crash or Yo-Yo Diets

Master cleanse. Cabbage soup. Grapefruit diet. Air.

If your teenager is constantly trying the next "proven" way to lose a quick ten pounds before an event or if your son or daughter is constantly overeating or eating poorly and then trying to drop a few pounds quickly so the cycle can be repeated, you've got a crash or yo-yo dieter.

According to recent studies, rapid weight loss can slow metabolism, causing increased weight gain, and it can deprive the body of essential nutrients. Crash diets can also weaken your immune system and increase your risk of dehydration, heart palpitations, and cardiac stress.[11] That's risking a lot of damage just to lose a few quick pounds.

There are times when rapid weight loss is safe—but it should always be under the supervision of a doctor, and except in extreme cases of morbid obesity, doctors would rarely recommend anything other than healthy eating and exercise for a teenager.

Signs your teen might be a crash or yo-yo dieter:

> Rigid list of allowable foods
> Changes diet plans regularly
> Overeats or eats poorly when not "on a diet"
> Has tried multiple diet plans, some with success
> Loses and gains weight regularly
> Doesn't eat enough calories

Other Disorders

There are many ways to practice disordered eating other than the ones listed above. Many teens enlist the help of diet pills or energy drinks to speed up the metabolism and curb the appetite. This is dangerous because it can cause a racing heart or increased blood pressure. The reduced caloric intake can slow the metabolism, leading to weight gain.

Extreme exercise can have addictive qualities that are dangerous to the body. Malnourishment, dehydration, muscle damage, heart damage, and blood pressure problems can all be caused by extremely excessive exercise. If you're unsure about the amount of exercise healthy for your teenager, check with the doctor for a safe plan.

As Mom and Dad, you know what's safe and logical for your tweens and teens. If you see behavior that makes you squirm, it's time to do some digging. Find out the cause of the changes and what the goal is so you can determine if it's a smart and healthy approach.

What causes an eating disorder?

The volatile period between 13 and 17 years old is full of hormonal, emotional, and physical changes. Peer pressure and the pressure to fit in by looking like everyone else can seem like crushing burdens to many teens and lead to eating disorders. They are common among teens who need to achieve and who chase after perfectionism. Many feel high amounts of pressure to succeed in school or at sports, and they are brutal to themselves if they fail.

When you combine the pressures tweens and teens face with the images with which the media bombards them on a daily basis, it's no wonder they feel inadequate. See the next chapter for more information about celebrity and media influence. In Hollywood, the girls are tiny and perky, and the boys are buff and hot. So your teens are wondering why they aren't tiny, hot, buff . . . or at least not quite to the same level as their favorite celebs.

Compounding factors like genetics, mental health, socioeconomic variables, faith, examples being set at home, and personal resolve all play a part in each teenager's risk of an eating disorder.[12]

The Effects of Eating Disorders

Eating disorders are serious illnesses and need to be treated medically and psychologically so they don't become lifelong battles that affect self-esteem and lead to even more dangerous behaviors like bullying, self-harm, and suicide.

Previously in this chapter, we went through the effects of some of the specific disorders, but in general any eating disorder can affect health by increasing the risk of:

- Heart attack
- Stroke
- Anemia (iron deficiency)
- Swollen joints
- Brittle bones
- Low circulation

The pain of an eating disorder affects the entire family. It can be exhausting and overwhelming to monitor caloric intake and to address areas of concern without causing your kids to pull away.

For your tweens and teens, an eating disorder can be completely debilitating as an inordinate amount of time gets used up in meal planning, binge planning, exercising, avoiding food, or avoiding social situations that involve food. Hiding a big secret like that is probably the most exhausting part of the problem.

Fortunately, eating disorders can be treated and sufferers can go on to lead normal, healthy lives. Counseling of some kind is usually necessary in order to uncover the root problem that led to the disordered eating. Therapy can help the teenager overcome the eating disorder and also help the support people identify the best ways to help without causing stumbling blocks.

Recommendations

Talk to your teens now and ask some pointed questions to determine their mental-health status in relation to eating disorders. Ask:

- Do you love your body?
- Do you worry about food intake at every meal? How about between meals?
- Have you ever made yourself throw up?
- How often do you regret what you eat?
- If you could change one thing about your body, what would it be?
- How badly do you want to change that feature?
- What can I do to help you feel better about yourself?

Moms and Dads, you set the tone in your home on the issue of true beauty and self-acceptance. Be sure you are modeling behaviors of loving your body, being happy with your weight, making healthy choices, and valuing true beauty over physical beauty.

It's so scary, Lord. I love my kids so much, and I just want them to know how great they are. The thought of them hating themselves or their bodies so much that they'd resort to destructive eating like this is so sad to me. Help me see the areas where I can build up my kids and show me where any dangers may already lurk. Help me let go of them enough that they can grow in You, but shelter them enough to protect them from their own mistakes and misconceptions. Please help me to see what I need to see and then respond in effective ways. And, Lord, please guard my tongue that I may never be the cause of any hurt in regard to my teenagers' individuality, self-worth, or physical appearance. Amen.

CHECK POINTS ➤➤➤

CHECK POINTS

✓ The most common eating disorders are anorexia and bulimia. There are many other ways to participate in disordered eating, like binge eating, food phobias, use of laxatives or diet pills, yo-yo dieting, and more.

✓ Many teens enlist the help of diet pills or energy drinks to speed up the metabolism and curb the appetite. This is dangerous because it can cause a racing heart or increased blood pressure. The reduced caloric intake can slow the metabolism, leading to weight gain.

✓ The volatile period between 13 and 17 years old is full of hormonal, emotional, and physical changes. Peer pressure and the pressure to fit in and look like everyone else can seem like crushing burdens to many teens.

✓ Eating disorders are serious illnesses and need to be treated medically and psychologically so they don't become lifelong battles that affect self-esteem and lead to even more dangerous behaviors like bullying, self-harm, and suicide.

✓ Moms and Dads, you set the tone in your home on the issue of true beauty and self-acceptance. Be sure you are modeling behaviors of loving your body, being happy with your weight, making healthy choices, and valuing true beauty over physical beauty.

Celebrities
& Media

I wonder if Mary of Nazareth was influenced by celebs and tried to look like them as much as today's teenagers do. Just the right hair under her scarf. Just the right sandals. How could she possibly work out enough to have legs like Herodias? Or diet enough to be skinny like a supermodel?

You don't think so? Why not?

One simple reason is that Mary didn't have much media access. Unlike Mary, we live in a time that places pictures, videos, articles, and gossip at our fingertips, a moment away. Gossip magazines pick apart our favorite celebrities and their famous body parts. We view them at the beach, in their homes, on television, in movies, and on the Internet. We learn about (and follow) news of their new and failed relationships, and word of their upcoming weddings and babies—hopefully in that order. We find out how much they weigh after giving birth, and how they shed the pounds in 2.4 weeks with the help of a fancy trainer and a fat vacuum. As a society, we scan for news of their one-night stands and friends-with-benefits situations. And then we can't wait to rake them over the coals of the red carpet with worst-dressed lists.

Mary? She didn't have access to any of that. And she had purpose. I'd like to think that she had more important things to worry about.

Celebrities influence fans to be destructively thin, put harmful substances in their bodies, and live a lifestyle far from the calling of God on the heart of a Christian. Some of the biggest areas of influence today's celebs have on our tweens and teens include:

- Physical appearance
- Plastic surgery and other artificial means of altering the body
- Immodest dress
- Focus on trends and name brands
- Drug use and alcohol abuse
- Drinking and driving, and other bad behaviors
- Lack of committed marriages
- Children outside of marriage

Here's a question for you, Mom and Dad. If a person in your neighborhood lived in such a way that the things from that list above could adequately describe his or her lifestyle, would you feel comfortable calling that person your best friend and asking for their help in raising your kids? Then why are we allowing celebrity strangers, who have lifestyles like those described, to have power and influence in our kids' lives?

Why follow celebrities?

Tweens and teens often fall for the glamour of celebrity and they want to look like those people they revere. They see picture-perfect bodies, living picture-perfect lives, in picture-perfect homes. What they don't realize, or fail to remember, is that every single one of those pictures is airbrushed. If we could have makeup artists, chefs, personal trainers, and airbrush experts following us around all day, every day, we could look like that too! With celebrities setting an impossibly high bar, and our tweens and teens feeling like they need to reach for that bar to have popularity, success, and happiness, we've got a problem.

If you read back through the chapters on topics like popularity, bullying, body image, and eating disorders, it's easy to see that our young people are having a hard time embracing the reality of who they are rather than falling for the ideal set forth by society. This is exactly why they chase so hard after celebrities.

In those celebs, our kids find proof that the ideal exists. And, here's the biggest component: Young people delude themselves into feeling a connection with those celebrities. With that connection, they feel the tingling of acceptance and popularity.

This is what drives them to know every detail about these celebrities. This is what drove my middle-school-aged daughter to not use a spoon for eight months. It's that desire for connection with perfection.

True story: My young daughter didn't use a spoon for eight months because a member of a boy band once said he was afraid of spoons. First of all, huh? Afraid of spoons? And this is the guy you think is so cool? So, then, what about him is so great?

It's not *who* he is; it's who everyone *else* thinks he is. If everyone thinks he's this superstar, and you're the girl who didn't use a spoon for eight months—even for soup or ice cream—then you're his biggest fan. You're the closest to him of anyone in school. You're the Superfan.

I'd like to blame this all on the media, but I can't. Honestly, looking back, the spoon thing seemed harmless. It was kind of funny to try to trick her into using a spoon—stick one into the soup and hope she grabbed it before she realized, hand her a bowl of ice cream and wait to see what she did. But she fooled us because . . . well . . . if you wait long enough, you can drink ice cream. But looking back, I believe I should have nipped the spoon thing in the bud.

Rather than letting my daughter focus on a spoon phobia as being a behavior to emulate in tribute to this boy, I wish I'd used that as a teaching moment. It seemed harmless, and perhaps it was with this daughter, but with some girls, the spoon would be a gateway to emulating drug and alcohol use or an eating disorder.

Based on a Kaiser Family Foundation survey, two out of three parents think their kids are exposed to too much inappropriate content in the media.[13] But my question is, why are they getting this exposure? Where are Mom and Dad while this is going on, and why are parents just sitting back and letting it happen?

The Consequences

Teens get so wrapped up in mimicking the behavior of celebrities, they forget to celebrate who they are themselves—beauty and imperfections aside, they want to look perfect and can't accept what's real. This dissatisfaction leads our young people to destructive behaviors that can have damaging effects.

For example, Ana Carolina Reston, a Brazilian model, died of anorexia at the age of twenty-one, weighing eighty-eight pounds. She was paid huge sums of money to keep her body rail thin in the name of so-called beauty, but she paid a huge price. But the part our teens internalize is that she was important and loved because she was skinny. They see that and dive into destructive eating habits as we discussed in the previous chapter.

At the other extreme, look at the media and public outcry over Jennifer Love Hewitt's bikini photo from 2012. She had put on a few pounds and looked—horror of horrors—like a real woman. But the media went crazy with cruel comments in response to her weight gain. Bloggers launched a feeding frenzy, attacking her body, her lifestyle, even her career.

For what reason? The size of her behind.

And who was watching? Our children.

If she is fat and ugly, what does that say about me?

And there we have it, Mom and Dad. The consequences of the two sides of the media hyper-focus on appearance. Both have an effect on our tweens and teens. Both extremes drive them to self-hate, destructive behaviors, and a false sense of beauty.

What can you do?

Well, you *can* throw out the television, stop going to the movies, shield your kids' eyes at the checkout stand, keep the radio off, get rid of the Internet. . . . Or, if that isn't possible, or seems futile, there are other steps you can take that will have longer-lasting effects and arm your kids with tools to take through all of life.

1. Time: The average teen girl gets about 180 minutes of media exposure daily and only about 10 minutes of parental interaction a day, says

Renee Hobbs, associate professor of communications at Temple University.[14] Do you plan time to spend with your tweens and teens? You need to be playing, laughing, sharing, talking, eating, and praying together. All of those things should be happening on a daily and weekly basis. There's no way all of that could fit into ten minutes. Give your kids the time they need apart from the influence of the media.

2. Talk: Do you talk to your kids about what's important to you, to them, and to God? Are you open about the influences of the media and do you talk about celebrity lifestyles and unrealistic ideals? Do you remind them regularly about how beautiful they are and what true beauty actually is? This goes back to number one, but it takes time to have these talks, so you have to be intentional about making that time.

3. Teach: Teach by modeling. Teach your teens what it means to enjoy acting talent and get lost in a good movie without becoming an obsessed fan. Don't reach for the gossip magazine the first chance you get, and be careful what you're watching on television. Your teens pay attention and they learn from the choices you make for yourself more than from the things you say.

Ultimately, Mom and Dad, you're the ones who set the tone in your home for dependence on or independence from media. You can and should set boundaries in place for what types of media are consumed, how often they are viewed or read, and who is followed or emulated. Role models are a good thing; just be sure that your tweens and teens are patterning their lives after people who are following God.

Jesus, there's just so much out there that can entice my teens and lead them down a dangerous path—when I think about it all, I feel sort of helpless. Please guide me. Help me to steer them well and love them through it all. Give me the words to say and the wisdom to see the truth of what's going on, the truth about what they're influenced by and what they try to emulate. Remove my blinders. I also ask for Your protection to surround my teenagers as they face the temptations and trappings of this world and the attacks of their enemy. Give them a full measure of Your wisdom as they face and respond to peer pressure. Thank You for loving them so much. Amen.

CHECK POINTS ➤➤➤

Celebrities & Media

CHECK POINTS

✓ Celebrities influence fans to be destructively thin, put harmful substances in their bodies, and live a lifestyle far from the calling of God.

✓ With celebrities setting an impossibly high bar, and our tweens and teens feeling like they need to reach for that bar to have popularity, success, and happiness, we've got a problem.

✓ In those celebs, our kids find proof that the ideal exists. And, here's the biggest component: Young people delude themselves into feeling a connection with those celebrities. With that connection, they feel the tingling of acceptance and popularity.

✓ Teens get so wrapped up in emulating celebrities, they forget to celebrate who they are themselves—beauty and imperfections aside, they want to look perfect and can't accept what's real. This dissatisfaction leads our young people to destructive behaviors that can have damaging effects.

✓ You need to be playing, laughing, sharing, talking, eating, and praying together. All of those things should be happening on a daily and weekly basis. There's no way all of that could fit into ten minutes. Give your kids the time they need apart from the influence of the media.

✓ Your teens pay attention and they learn from the choices you make for yourself more than from the things you say.

PART THREE

Pressing the Image HOT BUTTONS

"When you're different, sometimes you don't see the millions of people who accept you for what you are. All you notice is the person who doesn't."

—Jodi Picoult, CHANGE OF HEART

This is where the work comes in. You have the information you need; now you can put it into practice to really make a difference for your teens and your family. I encourage you to take every segment in the rest of this book very seriously—even if you've already seen something like it in other Hot Buttons books. The process may seem similar but the application of the specific concerns related to each issue is vital.

Practical Procedures

How hard are you willing to fight to make sure your tweens and teens have a righteous self-image? Are you willing to do what it takes to ensure they have a clear view of themselves the way God sees them and that they understand what's truly important? There are five aspects to successfully fighting the image battle (and all the parenting battles) in our teens' lives:

> ➤ Time
> ➤ Communication
> ➤ Example
> ➤ Consistency
> ➤ Prayer

Are you willing to put the time in to have the long talks, ask the hard questions, and explore the important truths about self-image? Are you modeling a healthy lifestyle and exhibiting a positive self-esteem, avoiding pitfalls like yo-yo dieting, and refusing to speak negatively about yourself? Then, once you've invested time and communication and are setting a positive example, you have to be consistent with your follow-up to make sure values are sticking after being tested by the real world, and consistent with your follow-through on consequences and promises. Last on the list but certainly not least in importance, are you bathing each child, each day with prayer, asking God to give you wisdom and clear vision as you lead them to a healthy self-image?

The Importance of a Good Example

We've talked about this quite a bit as we've gone through all of the hot-button issues, but this issue is most significant in relation to your child's self-image. It's so important that you're modeling healthy eating, regular exercise, and a good perspective on celebrity. It's vital that you're setting boundaries, and then proving their importance by living within them yourself. Acting on your values and being a good role model are powerful messages for your children. Your beliefs will not seem very important or valuable to your kids if they don't see you respect and abide by them yourself.

Girls, especially, take to heart what their mothers say about bodies: their own, their daughter's, those of strangers and celebrities. They notice when their mothers exercise obsessively, diet constantly, or make derogatory comments about their own appearance. That should come as no surprise, as Mom is a girl's first and, often, most influential role model.

Fathers play an equally important role in shaping their daughter's self-image. Girls listen first to what Daddy says and then subconsciously expect all males to see them the same way. If Dad is worried about his daughter's weight gain, she'll assume the boys at school are too. If she sees dad eyeing the women he encounters in public, she'll watch to see what attracted his attention and strive to attain that perception of beauty herself. That goes for comments about celebrities, too, Dad. Don't let your daughter be a media victim or your son become obsessed with being muscular or tough. Help them develop a healthy, realistic understanding that knows the secrets of airbrushing, stylists, trainers, plastic surgery, and other things that make celebrities seem perfect.

Finally, prayer and meditation in God's Word are the most important life skills you can model. Not only will they gird you up to be the parent you need to be but they will prepare your tweens and teens to receive your message. When they see you praying, you're modeling surrender and faith, which will help them trust you. Furthermore, they will trust God more easily when they know you've put all your trust in Him. But you can't just say that you do; you have to show it.

Parental Hotline

It's vital that you're a nonjudgmental listening ear. That doesn't mean that you can't call out what's right and wrong and identify what you know is best for your teen; it's not as much what you say as how you say it. Your teens should feel that, if nothing else, no matter how wrong they have been, you are a source of love and acceptance. You should lead them to forgiveness, not condemnation. Never doubt for one moment how much your children need a strong, healthy, and open relationship with you.

> **If they feel like you don't understand their feelings, they're far less likely to believe what you say about their worth and true beauty.**

Recommendations

Begin talking openly about this subject now.

Work through the Strategic Scenarios in chapter 11.

Talk over the topics in each chapter of this book and in *Hot Buttons Bullying Edition*.

Ask yourself some important questions:

> - Does my teen have a healthy self-image?
> - Does my child have a healthy understanding of celebrity?
> - Have I placed enough value on relationship with God rather than people?
> - Have I modeled a walk with Christ that displays a healthy self-esteem and a strong prayer life?

Help your teens open up to you by asking them safe questions like:

> - What do you see going on at your school in regard to body image?
> - Do you know people with eating disorders? What do you think about that?
> - Do you feel pressured to be thin or to dress just right?
> - Do you think peer pressure is a factor in the way you see yourself?
> - How much do you think celebrities influence your life?

Don't be afraid to pull back the reins a bit on media exposure.

Don't shame or belittle your teens into thinking insecurities are bad.

Discuss healthy self-esteem.

While the world laughs as we continue to abide by biblical standards, Christian parents must be willing to have uncomfortable conversations and make unpopular decisions in order to give our kids the best God has for them. We must be willing to stand up and shout *NO!* when the world tries to turn our children's eyes off of truth. It's our responsibility to raise them in the truth of God's Word and with a healthy respect for His creation—themselves.

CHECK POINTS ➤➤➤

CHECK POINTS

✓ It's vital that you're setting boundaries, and then proving their importance by living within them yourself. Acting on your values and being a good role model are powerful messages for your children.

✓ Fathers play an equally important role in shaping their daughter's self-image. Girls listen first to what Daddy says and then subconsciously expect all males to see them the same way.

✓ It's vital that you're a nonjudgmental listening ear. That doesn't mean that you can't call out what's right and wrong, and identify what you know is best for your teen; it's not as much what you say as how you say it.

✓ If they feel like you don't understand their feelings, they're far less likely to believe what you say about their worth and true beauty.

✓ Christian parents must be willing to have uncomfortable conversations and make unpopular decisions in order to give our kids the best God has for them.

✓ We must be willing to stand up and shout *NO!* when the world tries to turn our children's eyes off of truth. It's our responsibility to raise them in the truth of God's Word and with a healthy respect for His creation—themselves.

The Armor
of God

When dealing with self-esteem and image-related issues, the "armor of God" is not just some clever phrase in Scripture or a sermon illustration you might hear on a Sunday morning in church but a practical resource for navigating the spiritual battles Christ-followers face. The various parts of the armor of God equip and protect against the fiery darts of the enemy as he tries to destroy us and our children with lies about inadequacy, ugliness, loneliness, and worthlessness.

Before you move forward in this book as it guides you to attack the hot buttons of image head-on in the next few chapters, I want to lead you through a symbolic application of the armor of God. This exercise is meant to help you visualize the armor spelled out for us in Scripture. By physically displaying your use of that armor, you're stepping out in faith, believing that God's protection and provision are sufficient to meet your needs and your teens' needs. I do hope you'll take this section seriously even if you feel a little silly at times. It's not meant to be a trite exercise; it's a physical display of your faith in God's power and a symbol of your acceptance of His protections.

Below, you'll find a breakdown of Ephesians 6:10–17. Each phrase is followed by a bit of commentary and application, and a few directions.

Be strong in the Lord and in his mighty power. (Eph. 6:10)

Mom and Dad, you're not alone as you lead your children, and neither are they alone as they navigate the pressures of self-image. All of the strength and wisdom you need to be a godly parent is already yours through the power of the Lord. You don't have to have all of the answers—He does. You don't have to see the future—He does. You don't have to make up for past hurts and insecurities—He did.

Do this: Raise your open hands in surrender, ready to receive from God and expectant that He'll grant you strength, wisdom, and grace.

Pray this: *Lord, please help me stand strong in the power of Your might. Help me to let go of my worry that my child will get swallowed by the need to please others and gain their approval, and make it possible for me to surrender my family to You. Let me rest in Your power, and walk as a parent in Your strength. Guide my senses with Your knowledge and help me to know what I need to, when I need to, especially as it pertains to what my teens believe about themselves.*

Put on the full armor of God, so that you can take your stand against the devil's schemes. (Eph. 6:11)

God has already provided your protection against the enemy in the form of armor. He has already secured your ultimate victory in the parenting battle—even if it seems daunting at times. Remember the promise in Philippians 1:6, where it says that He started the work (in your teens), and He'll finish it. He stands ready to uphold you as you face the enemy that seeks to pull your teens down that slippery slope of not-good-enough.

Do this: Stand strong. Confident. Stand proud like a soldier waiting for orders. Ultimately, as parents we are constantly waiting for divine direction, like a ready soldier.

Pray this: *Lord, please prepare my body to receive Your armor. Place it carefully that I might be protected as a parent from doubt, fear, and other attacks of the enemy. Then, protect my teens in the same way, Father—their eyes, hands, mouths, and bodies . . . and guard them from false expectations of themselves. Let them run from danger and stand strong against temptation when it comes to the issues surrounding their self-esteem.*

For **our struggle is not against flesh and blood**, but against the rulers, against the authorities, against the powers of this dark world and **against the spiritual forces of evil** in the heavenly realms. (Eph. 6:12)

You see, your real fight isn't against the popular kids or the bullies. It isn't against the rich kids or the partiers. And it definitely isn't against your teenagers. It's against the enemy who seeks to destroy.

Do this: Place your hands on your child's bedroom or bathroom door.

Pray this: *Father, I surrender this child, whom You love with a passion far greater than even I, to You. I call on Your mighty power to fight against our enemy who has no place in this family. We choose this day whom we will serve and I claim Your promises over the inhabitants of this home that no stronghold of low self-esteem or poor body image will take captive a child of God in this home.*

Therefore put on **the full armor of God**, so that when **the day of evil comes**, you may be able to **stand your ground**, and after you have done everything, to stand. (Eph. 6:13)

Armor is the barricade between the enemy's lies, and your heart, mind, and body. With the armor of God in place, Satan is eternally powerless against you, and by extension, your teenagers, because, as Christians, we know how the story ends. We may feel like we lose some of the battles along the way; we might get discouraged at times. But in the end, we win! We can rest in the promise that God will complete the work He began in us and in our teens, even if we don't see that completion until we stand before Him one day.

Do this: Close your eyes and imagine impenetrable steel covering every inch of your body and your teen's body.

Pray this: *With armor in place, I stand proud as a soldier fighting for my family. I visualize the armor covering my child's head, heart, and soul.*

I stand confident in Your assurances of spiritual protection, physical guidance, and eternal completion.

Stand firm then, with **the belt of truth** buckled around your waist . . . (Eph. 6:14a)

Do this: Buckle a proverbial belt around your waist. Then do the same in front of you as though your teens are present.

Pray this: *With your truth around our waists, let it restrain our fleshly desires and poor choices and lead us on Your path. Let Your truth penetrate through the lies and reveal our image through Your eyes.*

. . . with the **breastplate of righteousness** in place . . . (Eph. 6:14b)

The breastplate provides protection for the heart and lungs, and without it, a solider is asking for death. A good breastplate wards off the attacks of the enemy, just as righteousness wards off the attacks of Satan.

Do this: Move your hands in front of your body and in front of you, representing your kids.

Pray this: *Let Your righteousness, Lord, be a shield about this family. Our protector and the lifter of our heads. Let Your armor protect my* *teen from the lies of the enemy and the temptation to chase after the approval of others.*

. . . and with your **feet fitted with the readiness** that comes **from the gospel of peace**. (Eph. 6:15)

You're ready. You have the information you need and you're covered in prayer. In the next chapters, you're going to actually implement the principles of getting and staying battle ready.

Do this: Lift each foot and plant it down hard.

Pray this: *I trust You, Jesus. I am confident in Your Word. I believe that You have led me and prepared me to be my teens' very best advocate in this world. I am prepared to fight as Your ambassador, ready to defend.*

In addition to all this, **take up the shield of faith**, with which you can extinguish all the flaming arrows of the evil one. (Eph. 6:16)

Notice, the shield is active, not simply defensive. You're not blocking the enemy's arrows and sending them back out to do damage somewhere else; you're extinguishing them. Apply that to the evil that lurks around the corner and the lies being thrown at your kids about their self-worth.

Do this: Raise your arm as though you hold a shield and wave it in front of you. Imagine your kids standing before you, and wave it in front of each of them also.

Pray this: *Put out the flames, Lord. Let this shield of my faith swallow them whole that they would disappear, never to harm another soul again. And may You strengthen my children that they would hold their shield in place, fending off the darts of the enemy.*

Take the **helmet of salvation** . . . (Eph. 6:17a)

The helmet protects your mind from doubt, fear, anger, apathy, jealousy, and false expectations.

Do this: Place the helmet of salvation securely over your head, to your shoulders. Reach out in front of you and do the same as though your teens stood before you.

Pray this: *I rest in my salvation, Lord. You are mighty to save and faithful to preserve Your children.*

. . . and the **sword of the Spirit**, which is the word of God. (Eph. 6:17b)

The Armor of God

You're armed and ready to fight. In the following chapters, I will walk you through the next action steps in your battle for your tweens and teens.

Do this: Raise your sword, which is the Bible—the Word of God.

Pray this: *I am equipped and ready to fight Satan's schemes against my kids. But I need You, Lord, to guide me and show me what my next move should be. Keep my heart and mind open to the truths and possibilities of what my kids face. And help them, Lord, to have the strength to reject the words of the evil one, the wisdom to walk away from temptation and peer pressure, and the passion to chase hard after You. Amen.*

———————————————

chapter 11

Strategic Scenarios

The first few chapters of this book identified why it's necessary to press the hot buttons with your teens about image and all that comes along with that topic. Part 2 outlined the specific segments of the issues like body image, self-esteem, eating disorders, and the effect celebrities and media have on self-image. Now we're going to actually implement strategies to affect real change and a lasting impact.

Desiring the approval of others is one of the basic designs of human nature. We're relational beings, and we want to connect with people we respect. That's not going to change, and it can't be ignored. It's also not an issue your teen can figure out alone. Don't leave this one to chance, parents. Invest time with your children and reap the rewards.

Putting the Strategic Scenarios into practice will involve placing your tween or teen into a scenario by telling a short story. You'll then present a few optional responses to the situation from which you'll allow your child to choose the most natural personal choice without any judgment. Once that decision is made, you'll be guided to lead your teen through several discussion points, and referred back to material given previously in this book.

Each discussion will end with the opportunity for your son or daughter to change that initial decision and commit to wise choices in the future.

Some of the scenarios are written from the perspective of a particular gender. You should still guide your tween or teen through those scenarios, either modifying the scenario to match your child's gender, or helping him or her see the particular difficulties experienced by the opposite gender. Many times they will learn more from the opposite perspective, and identify issues they see in the lives of their peers, so don't skip over scenarios that don't seem to apply. This is about equipping your tweens and teens with the tools for making good choices, so that when the need arises, they are prepared.

Parents, tell your teen this story.

One of your friends is kind of unpopular at school. The boys make fun of her because she's a little fat and has funny hair. She hasn't been doing her homework lately and her grades are falling. She's about to get into big trouble with her parents, but she said she doesn't care. She said she might not stick around to get punished and that, "There's no point in being here when you're ugly and have no friends." What do you do?

Now offer the following options with no personal commentary.

Let your teen think about the choices and make an honest decision.

> A. You thank God that you're more popular and attractive than she is and hope she doesn't do anything stupid.
>
> B. You tell her she must be blind and that she's prettier than she thinks. Hopefully that'll be enough to keep her from thinking more thoughts like that.
>
> C. You have a long talk with her about how important she is to you and that you're scared she's going to do something crazy. You offer to help her get her grades back up.
>
> D. You talk to your parents or her parents immediately.

Crucial Step

Use this scenario to guide a discussion about self-esteem and suicidal tendencies. Be very careful not to sound judgmental or accusatory. Remember, your teen is exploring thoughts and first impressions—these aren't actual choices . . . yet.

Discussion Points

- Why did you make the choice you did?
- What are some warning signs of possible suicide?
- How would you feel in this situation?
- What does God think of this girl?
- How should this girl handle the situation? What should her focus be?
- What are some other ways you can help?
- Practice the dialogue you might have with her parents if you needed to talk with them.
- Do you now have a different view on this scenario than you did at the start? Why or why not?
- Would you like to change your answer or stick with it?

Finally, brothers and sisters, **whatever is true**, whatever is **noble**, whatever is **right**, whatever is **pure**, whatever is **lovely**, whatever is **admirable**—if anything is excellent or praiseworthy— **think about such things**. Whatever you have learned or received or heard from me, or seen in me—put it into practice. **And the God of peace will be with you**.

(Phil. 4:8–9)

Parents, tell your teen this story.

You're at the mall with a friend and about to eat in the food court. She reaches her cup out to fill it with soda at the pop machine. Her sleeve shifts up and you notice a row of four purple bruises on her forearm. You grab her arm and ask what happened—even though you already have a pretty good idea, considering who her boyfriend is. She says she bumped into something and that it was nothing to worry about. You press her until she admits that her boyfriend grabbed her and shoved her a few days ago. She assures you that it's the first time anything like this has ever happened and that he promised it wouldn't happen again. What do you do?

Now offer the following options with no personal commentary.

Let your teen think about the choices and make an honest decision.

> A. You give her a phone number for a hotline to call if she ever feels in danger.
>
> B. Well, maybe he's changed. As long as he keeps his promise, it'll be okay.
>
> C. What can you do? If she's stupid enough to believe him, that's her problem.
>
> D. You tell her she needs to break up with him or you'll have to tell her parents.

Crucial Step

Use this scenario to guide a discussion about self-esteem and dating violence. Be very careful not to sound judgmental or accusatory. Remember, your teen is exploring thoughts and first impressions—these aren't actual choices . . . yet.

Discussion Points

- Why did you make the choice you did?
- What is the big danger in this situation?
- Should she forgive him?
- Should she believe his promises and stay in the relationship?
- Are those two questions the same thing? Does forgiveness require blind trust?
- How far does physical anger have to go to be considered abuse?
- What does this scenario have to do with self-esteem?
- What possible problems might there be with option D? How could you make it an even better choice?
- Do you now have a different view on this scenario than you did at the start? Why or why not?
- Would you like to change your answer or stick with it?

Are not five sparrows sold for two pennies? **Yet not one of them is forgotten by God**. Indeed, the very hairs of your head are all numbered. **Don't be afraid; you are worth more than many sparrows**.

(Luke 12:6–7)

Parents, tell your teen this story.

Big party this weekend! All of your friends are going and they're all wearing something new and fabulous. Problem is, you don't have the money to buy new clothes by this weekend. If you don't wear a new outfit, you'll be proving to everyone that you're poor. But the only way to get something new would be to steal it, or maybe you can steal some of the grocery money from Mom's purse. It wouldn't be the first time. What do you do?

Now offer the following options with no personal commentary.

Let your teen think about the choices and make an honest decision.

> A. You're going to that party, and you're wearing a new outfit. Problem is, Mom would know the money is missing. You find a way to steal a new top and pair of jeans from your favorite store.
>
> B. You go to the party wearing an outfit you already own.
>
> C. You have plenty of jeans, so a new shirt would be enough. You steal thirty dollars from your mom's purse. That should cover it.
>
> D. You tell your friends you can't go to the party. At least you won't have to sit face-to-face with the reminder.

Crucial Step

Use this scenario to guide a discussion about trends and pressure to conform. Be very careful not to sound judgmental or accusatory. Remember, your teen is exploring thoughts and first impressions—these aren't actual choices . . . yet.

Discussion Points

- Why did you make the choice you did?
- Do real friends care if your clothes are new? What should real friends care about?
- What lie from the enemy might be behind the struggle to make a good decision on this?
- Is stealing ever an acceptable option?
- Is popularity or approval worth risking your parents' trust? Is it worth risking arrest?
- If one of your friends showed up in a preworn outfit, would you judge her?
- Is there a better choice than any of those listed above?
- Do you now have a different view on this scenario than you did at the start? Why or why not?
- Would you like to change your answer or stick with it?

Your beauty should not come from outward adornment, such as elaborate hairstyles and the wearing of gold jewelry or fine clothes. **Rather, it should be that of your inner self**, the unfading beauty of a gentle and quiet spirit, **which is of great worth in God's sight**. (1 Peter 3:3–4)

Parents, tell your teen this story.

Two girls have been after you for a while. You like them both, so how do you decide? One of them dresses modestly and goes to church, but she isn't as pretty as the other one who wears the trendiest clothes and parties hard. You like the first girl, but your friends would think you're crazy for not going for the hot, fun girl. What do you do?

Now offer the following options with no personal commentary.

Let your teen think about the choices and make an honest decision.

A. You pick the modest girl who goes to church. You like her more and you're attracted to her values. Who cares what your friends say?

B. You only live once, and it's high school. You're going out with the hot girl who wears clothes that highlight all her best features.

C. What if you go out with both of them? You don't have to tell them, at least not right away. Then your friends will think you're an animal.

D. You don't go out with either of them. Girls are expensive and it's too hard to make a decision.

Crucial Step

Use this scenario to guide a discussion about dating choices. Be very careful not to sound judgmental or accusatory. Remember, your teen is exploring thoughts and first impressions—these aren't actual choices . . . yet.

Discussion Points

- Why did you make the choice you did?
- How does the way a girl dresses affect a boy?
- How do style and modesty affect your opinion about someone?
- If you choose to pursue a relationship based on physical attraction, what's the likely outcome?
- The hard thing is often the right thing.
- Do you want to be a strong, confident person, or do you want to be a follower and a people pleaser?
- Do you now have a different view on this scenario than you did at the start? Why or why not?
- Would you like to change your answer or stick with it?

Charm is deceitful, and beauty is vain, but **a woman who fears the LORD is to be praised**. (Prov. 31:30 ESV)

Parents, tell your teen this story.

Your mom found the coolest formal dress on eBay. It's actually the dress a celebrity wore on the red carpet. Problem is, it's a bit too small, and you know there's no way you will fit into it unless you drop ten pounds fast. You only have a week, but you have to do it because everyone's been talking about you wearing this dress. If you don't, they'll know it's because you're too fat. What do you do?

Now offer the following options with no personal commentary.

Let your teen think about the choices and make an honest decision.

> A. You diet as best you can, but eventually you take the dress to a tailor. Surely something can be done.
>
> B. You do whatever it takes. You stop eating, but when you cheat, you just make yourself throw up.
>
> C. You eat nothing but apples and water, and work out three hours a day.
>
> D. A week isn't enough time to lose weight safely. You find a different dress to wear.

Crucial Step

Use this scenario to guide a discussion about healthy weight loss and body image. Be very careful not to sound judgmental or accusatory. Remember, your teen is exploring thoughts and first impressions—these aren't actual choices . . . yet.

Discussion Points

- Why did you make the choice you did?
- Describe a healthy way to lose weight.
- What's better: a crash diet or a healthy lifestyle?
- See chapter 6 for discussions about eating disorders and the effects diets have on the body.
- What would you say to a friend in this situation?
- How does this relate to self-esteem?
- Do you now have a different view on this scenario than you did at the start? Why or why not?
- Would you like to change your answer or stick with it?

Do you not know that **your bodies are temples of the Holy Spirit**, who is in you, whom you have received from God? You are not your own; you were bought at a price. **Therefore honor God with your bodies**.

(1 Cor. 6:19–20)

Parents, tell your teen this story.

Your parents have rules about the kind of clothes you're allowed to wear. They have to be a certain length and have to meet several other standards as well—can't ride up in the back, can't be low-cut, and can't show stomach. But your friends all think you dress like an old lady and they say you need to amp up your look if you want to keep hanging out with them. What do you do?

Now offer the following options with no personal commentary.

Let your teen think about the choices and make an honest decision.

> A. You tell your friends that real friends wouldn't say those things and that you think your parents are right to promote modesty.
>
> B. You leave the house in the clothes that make Mom happy, and then change on the bus by rolling up your skirt or unbuttoning your shirt a bit.
>
> C. You hide clothes in your locker and change at school.
>
> D. You tell your friends you aren't going to change and hope they'll drop it.

Crucial Step

Use this scenario to guide a discussion about modesty and peer pressure. Be very careful not to sound judgmental or accusatory. Remember, your teen is exploring thoughts and first impressions—these aren't actual choices . . . yet.

Discussion Points

- Why did you make the choice you did?
- What is modesty?
- What are the benefits of modesty to your reputation and your future?
- How is this a self-esteem issue?
- What would a real friend expect about how a person dresses?
- What are the rules for clothing in your home?
- Do you agree with the rules or do you struggle with them?
- Do you now have a different view on this scenario than you did at the start? Why or why not?
- Would you like to change your answer or stick with it?

I also want the women to **dress modestly, with decency and propriety**, adorning themselves, not with elaborate hairstyles or gold or pearls or expensive clothes . . .

(1 Tim. 2:9)

Parents, tell your teen this story.

Your breasts are way more developed than your friends' are and you get teased a lot. Boys whistle and girls stare; it's the worst during gym class when it's time to change clothes. You never go to the beach or to any events that involve swimsuits because they're too revealing. Just today you discovered that someone posted on Facebook that you had breast enlargement surgery. They even have falsified before and after pictures. What do you do?

Now offer the following options with no personal commentary.

Let your teen think about the choices and make an honest decision.

A. You beg your parents to move to Alaska to live with the Eskimos so you can avoid the kids at school and you can wear a parka all the time.

B. You start saving for breast-reduction surgery and retaliate on Facebook.

C. You ignore the taunts and the Facebook post. Eventually it'll stop.

D. You talk to your parents about the bullying you're enduring.

Crucial Step

Use this scenario to guide a discussion about body image and cyberbullying. Be very careful not to sound judgmental or accusatory. Remember, your teen is exploring thoughts and first impressions—these aren't actual choices . . . yet.

Discussion Points

- Why did you make the choice you did?
- Is this bullying? Why or why not?
- Parents, see *Hot Buttons Bullying Edition* for more information.
- Should you hide away because of your body?
- What is the wrongdoing in this scenario? Should you allow that to control your life?
- Discuss flattering and modest ways to dress to minimize body parts.
- What would you say to a friend if this were happening to her?
- Do you now have a different view on this scenario than you did at the start? Why or why not?
- Would you like to change your answer or stick with it?

For **we are** his workmanship, **created in Christ Jesus for good works**, which God prepared beforehand, that we should walk in them.

(Eph. 2:10 ESV)

Strategic Scenario 8

You are hanging out with your best friends—you've been friends with these guys since elementary school. A new kid walks by—he's kind of small and, well, sort of a geek. Your friends start giving him a hard time. They call him "little girl" and other hurtful things. One actually shoves the boy's books from his hands. What do you do?

Now offer the following options with no personal commentary.

Let your teen think about the choices and make an honest decision.

> A. You help the boy pick up his books, and laugh about it. Since you're laughing, your friends should be fine with it.
>
> B. Do? You didn't do anything wrong and you're not going to pick sides with the new kid over your best friends. You do nothing.
>
> C. You don't want to pick a fight, so you offer the boy a slight smile as he walks away. You hope your friends didn't see it.
>
> D. You tell your friends they are way out of line to treat him that way. You help the boy pick up his books and then walk off with him to help him find his next class.

Crucial Step

Use this scenario to guide a discussion about self-confidence and bullying. Be very careful not to sound judgmental or accusatory. Remember, your teen is exploring thoughts and first impressions—these aren't actual choices . . . yet.

Discussion Points

- How do you feel about this story?
- Should you say something to stop the bullying? What's at risk if you do?
- What if it happened again? What's at risk if you don't do anything?
- Parents, see *Hot Buttons Bullying Edition* for more help.
- How does this relate to body image or self-esteem?
- How would you feel if it were you being harassed?
- Do you now have a different view on this scenario than you did at the start? Why or why not?
- Would you like to change your answer or stick with it?

Defend the weak and the fatherless; uphold the cause of **the poor** and **the oppressed.**

(Ps. 82:3)

Parents, tell your teen this story.

You've been dating a boy for a few months—someone you've had a crush on forever who happens to be one of the most popular boys in school. Things are going great; you might even love him, except when he gets mad. He loses his temper every few weeks and things get ugly. You've managed to get out of arguing with him by going home or leaving wherever you are, but the other night, you weren't so lucky. He screamed at you that you weren't worth his time and shoved you to the ground. Later he cried and begged you to forgive him. He promised he'd never, ever yell at you or push you again. What do you do?

Now offer the following options with no personal commentary.

Let your teen think about the choices and make an honest decision.

A. You dump him and tell your parents what happened.

B. It's not like you're perfect. Everyone has a flaw. You'll just help him work through his.

C. You can't leave him. Who would date you if you dumped one of the most popular boys in school?

D. You tell him you need a little break, but that once you get your thoughts together, you want to pick up where you left off.

Crucial Step

Use this scenario to guide a discussion about dating violence. Be very careful not to sound judgmental or accusatory. Remember, your teen is exploring thoughts and first impressions—these aren't actual choices . . . yet.

Discussion Points

- Why did you make the choice you did?
- What is the big danger in this situation?
- What do you expect would happen if you stayed with him?
- How far does physical anger have to go to be considered abuse?
- What type of self-esteem issues would keep a girl with someone like this?
- Boundaries are healthy and need to be respected.
- What would you expect your parents to do in response to this?
- Do you agree their actions would be necessary? Why or why not?
- Do you now have a different view on this scenario than you did at the start? Why or why not?
- Would you like to change your answer or stick with it?

Wise friends make you wise, but you hurt yourself by going around with fools.
(Prov. 13:20 CEV)

Strategic Scenario 10

Parents, tell your teen this story.

Lately your BFF has been changing. She's listening to different music and wearing different clothes. She's becoming kind of emo and hanging out with other kids from that group. She says she still wants to be friends with you—that it's just her style that's changed a bit, not her—but you aren't sure what to do. If you hang out with her, it might jeopardize your position in your current group of friends. Is that a risk you want to take? What do you do?

Now offer the following options with no personal commentary.

Let your teen think about the choices and make an honest decision.

> A. Maybe you can hang out with her kind of secretly, like at night and on the weekends, but not at school.
>
> B. It looks interesting. You decide to follow her to the new group.
>
> C. She's your BFF. It doesn't matter what she looks like or how she dresses, you remain loyal to her.
>
> D. You can't risk it. If she's going to go that route, she'll have to go it alone.

Crucial Step

Use this scenario to begin a discussion about popularity and loyalty. Be very careful not to sound judgmental or accusatory. Remember, your teen is exploring thoughts and first impressions—these aren't actual choices . . . yet.

Discussion Points

- Why did you make the choice you did?
- What is the basis for true friendship?
- Does personal style always translate to behavior?
- Do you really want to be friends with people who make you reject someone else?
- What is something else you should probably consider about your friend?
- How much do clothing and appearance play a role in friendships at your school?
- Do you now have a different view on this scenario than you did at the start? Why or why not?
- Would you like to change your answer or stick with it?

Be careful to **live properly** among your unbelieving neighbors. Then even if they accuse you of doing wrong, **they will see your honorable behavior**, and they will give honor to God when he judges the world. (1 Peter 2:12 NLT)

Parents, tell your teen this story.

Your class is putting on a play for the school and community. You have to participate for a grade, but the teacher is letting each student choose whether to play an acting role, or to help out behind the scenes. You really want to try out for a role, and you've already memorized the lead, but your friends have started teasing you about it. They'll never let you live it down if you act in the play. What do you do?

Now offer the following options with no personal commentary.

Let your teen think about the choices and make an honest decision.

> A. You are going for the lead no matter what the others think.
> B. You take a backstage job. It's not worth getting hassled about.
> C. You take a backstage job but secretly hope the lead actor gets pneumonia or something so you can step in at the last minute to play the part.
> D. You try out for the acting role, get the lead, and then turn it down before your friends find out. At least you know you could have gotten it.

Crucial Step

Use this scenario to guide a discussion about being true to yourself. Be very careful not to sound judgmental or accusatory. Remember, your teen is exploring thoughts and first impressions—these aren't actual choices . . . yet.

Discussion Points

- Why did you make the choice you did?
- What does it mean to be true to yourself?
- Why would friends tease another friend about something like this?
- How is this a self-esteem issue?
- What are some of your interests that you keep hidden from the kids at school? Why?
- How can Mom and Dad help you realize those dreams?
- Do you now have a different view on this scenario than you did at the start? Why or why not?
- Would you like to change your answer or stick with it?

Do not conform to the pattern of this world, but **be transformed by the renewing of your mind**. Then you will be able to test and approve what God's will is—his good, pleasing and perfect will.

(Rom. 12:2)

Parents, tell your teen this story.

You are in love with someone, and you want to marry him. You'll have three kids, live in a big house, have two dogs, and take vacations all over the world. You already have your wedding dress picked out and the honeymoon planned. You're going to get married in a private villa on an island with fifty of your closest friends and then come home to have a raging reception a week later. Problem is, he has no idea you exist and he has three million other girls who want to marry him. What do you do?

Now offer the following options with no personal commentary.

Let your teen think about the choices and make an honest decision.

> A. You search online for tickets and backstage passes to his next show. Now, how to raise five hundred dollars?
>
> B. If you're ever going to rise above fan-girl status, you're going to have to do something crazy like send him a topless picture.
>
> C. You know you won't get married, but you're going to enjoy your fascination, or sick obsession, a while longer.
>
> D. It's time to move on. You take the posters off the wall and put away the sheet set and comforter with his face all over it.

Crucial Step

Use this scenario to guide a discussion about celebrity crushes. Be very careful not to sound judgmental or accusatory. Remember, your teen is exploring thoughts and first impressions—these aren't actual choices . . . yet.

Discussion Points

- Why did you make the choice you did?
- What is a fan girl?
- What is it about celebrities that make fans so committed and focused?
- Should you hold out hope or let go?
- How do your parents feel about your obsession?
- Can you back off from it? What would be most difficult to let go of?
- Are you afraid of being alone, even in your mind?
- How is this a self-esteem issue?
- Do you now have a different view on this scenario than you did at the start? Why or why not?
- Would you like to change your answer or stick with it?

When I was a child, I spoke and thought and reasoned as a child. But **when I grew up, I put away childish things**.

(1 Cor. 13:11 NLT)

Parents, tell your teen this story.

You're at a party and some girls from school start dancing on a table and taking off their shirts. Some of the guys are giving them dollars. Everyone is screaming and cheering. Your good friends even give money to the girls. What do you do?

Now offer the following options with no personal commentary.

Let your teen think about the choices and make an honest decision.

> A. You go into another room until things settle down.
> B. You tell your friends that the way they treated those girls was wrong and ask them to apologize for celebrating the girls' shame.
> C. You stick a couple of dollars in the girls' pockets. No reason you shouldn't have fun, too.
> D. You leave the party and go home. It's not your thing, but you're not going to judge the others.

Crucial Step

Use this scenario to guide a discussion about modesty and objectifying. Be very careful not to sound judgmental or accusatory. Remember, your teen is exploring thoughts and first impressions—these aren't actual choices . . . yet.

Discussion Points

- Why did you make the choice you did?
- Who was wrong in this scenario?
- Were the girls victims?
- What does it mean to objectify a girl?
- How is this a self-esteem issue for the girls? How about the boys?
- How could you be an example of Jesus Christ in this scenario?
- Would you tell your parents? Why or why not?
- In this case, who has the right to know?
- Do you now have a different view on this scenario than you did at the start? Why or why not?
- Would you like to change your answer or stick with it?

No temptation has overtaken you except what is common to mankind. And **God is faithful**; he will not let you be tempted beyond what you can bear. But **when you are tempted, he will also provide a way out** so that you can endure it.

(1 Cor. 10:13)

Parents, tell your teen this story.

Your best friend has been losing a lot of weight. At first she was looking really great, but lately she's becoming so skinny. Her face looks really tired and her eyes look kind of sunk into her head. Her wrist bones are even sticking out. You really think she's in trouble, but she won't listen no matter how many times you've tried to reach out to her. She says she doesn't have a problem, and that she's not even trying to lose weight. But you never see her eat. What do you do?

Now offer the following options with no personal commentary.

Let your teen think about the choices and make an honest decision.

A. You sneak protein powder into her water bottle.

B. You've tried to talk to her, and you probably will again, but there's nothing more you can do.

C. You get a group of friends to sign a petition to make her eat.

D. Her life is in danger, and you know this is more than you can handle on your own. You reach out to your parents for help.

Crucial Step

Use this scenario to guide a discussion about eating disorders. Be very careful not to sound judgmental or accusatory. Remember, your teen is exploring thoughts and first impressions—these aren't actual choices . . . yet.

Discussion Points

- Why did you make the choice you did?
- Why is this a dangerous situation?
- Read and discuss chapter 6 on eating disorders.
- What could be driving her to lose this much weight?
- How would you want someone to help you?
- Mom, Dad, what would you do if your teenager brought this situation to your attention?
- Teenager, how do you feel about that?
- How can you share God's love in this situation?
- Do you now have a different view on this scenario than you did at the start? Why or why not?
- Would you like to change your answer or stick with it?

I praise you, for **I am fearfully and wonderfully made**. Wonderful are your works; my soul knows it very well.

(Ps. 139:14 ESV)

Parents, tell your teen this story.

You've been popular since you were young. It's been kind of a hard thing to maintain because you have to watch everything you do. Your friends want you to be a certain way, and the other kids, who just want to be your friends, expect you to be better than them. It's a lot of pressure. You're always on a diet. You can never just relax and have fun without worrying. You can't even be friends with the people you want to be friends with. In fact, there's a new kid in school who seems really nice. But your friends have already decided that none of you can befriend the new kid. What do you do?

Now offer the following options with no personal commentary.

Let your teen think about the choices and make an honest decision.

A. Right or wrong, you've worked too hard to become popular. You're not giving it up now. You do what your friends say.

B. It's time you stood up for yourself. You invite the new kid to eat at your lunch table.

C. You want to be friends with this new kid, but maybe you can do it in secret. You wait until after school and send a Facebook message.

D. You work it out so you have to be partners with the new student on a science project. That will give you the chance to see if a friendship would be worth the risk.

Crucial Step

Use this scenario to guide a discussion about popularity and friendship and being yourself. Be very careful not to sound judgmental or accusatory. Remember, your teen is exploring thoughts and first impressions—these aren't actual choices . . . yet.

Discussion Points

- Why did you make the choice you did?
- How important is popularity to you?
- Popularity probably starts just because someone is nice and fun to be around. When does that change so that others control the popular kid's actions?
- What kind of friends would put these limits on someone?
- How common is this kind of behavior in your school? How do you respond to it?
- How would you feel if you were the shunned new student?
- Do you now have a different view on this scenario than you did at the start? Why or why not?
- Would you like to change your answer or stick with it?

> **Do nothing from selfish ambition** or conceit, but in humility count others more significant than yourselves. **Let each of you look** not only to his own interests, but also **to the interests of others**.
>
> (Phil. 2:3-4 ESV)

PART FOUR

Parent-Teen
STUDY
GUIDE

Congratulations on making it this far through *Hot Buttons Image Edition!* This book has dealt with some tough issues and walked you through the practice of using Strategic Scenarios to prepare your teens for the issues related to self-image. Now we're going to press in a little deeper and do some work on the spiritual side of choices: sin, confession, and forgiveness.

No matter what the ages of your children are, you'll find some common ground and will learn something about each other through these studies. You might want to pull them out every six months or year to see if things have changed and to make sure you're still working toward the same goals. You may verbalize your discussion, write it in a notebook, or utilize the free downloadable study guide, which you can find at www.hotbuttonsite.com/study-guide.

And, please, if you've already worked through these study chapters in another Hot Buttons book, go ahead and do them again. There's no better way to really learn, really internalize something than to repeat it. And I'm sure that the study of image and its effects on the heart and mind has raised questions, doubts, and fears. This is where you'll deal with all of that.

Confession 12

Very **truly I tell you**, the one who **believes** has eternal life. (John 6:47)

. . . **Jesus is the Messiah**, the Son of God, and that **by _believing_** you may have life in his name. (John 20:31)

Jesus said to her, "I am the resurrection and the life. The one **who _believes_ in me will live**, even though they die; and whoever lives by believing in me will never die. Do you _believe_ this?" (John 11:25–26)

If you **confess with your mouth Jesus as Lord**, and **_believe_ in your heart** that God raised Him from the dead, **you will be saved**; for with the heart a person _believes_, resulting in righteousness, and with the mouth he confesses, resulting in salvation. (Rom. 10:9–10 NASB)

◀ According to these verses, what is required for salvation?

Stop and think. Have you confessed with your mouth and believed in your heart that Jesus is Lord? Share the answer with your study partner(s).

◀ What does that mean to you to have made that choice?

If you haven't done that but would like to now, take a walk through the following Scriptures. If you're a Christian already, it's still a good exercise to look at these foundational truths as a refresher.

◀ Read Romans 3:23. Who has sinned?

◀ Read Romans 6:23a. What is the price of sin?

Sin requires a penalty. The only payment for it is death, blood. Worse than a physical death, though, is the spiritual death that separates us from God for eternity.

◀ Read Romans 6:23b. What is God's gift?

◀ Read Romans 5:8. How much does God love you?

Jesus gave His own life on the cross to pay the penalty for all of our sin. He, an innocent man, took your death sentence and stood in your place, giving you new life in exchange for His death.

◀ Read Romans 10:13 and Revelation 3:20. Who qualifies for salvation?

If you'd like to welcome Jesus into your life and receive the free gift of eternal life that He offers, simply pray this prayer:

> *Dear Jesus, I believe in You. I believe that You are the Son of God and my Savior and Lord. I ask You to forgive my sins and make*

Confession

me clean. Please help me do the right thing, but I thank You for the forgiveness You offer me when I mess up. I give my life to You. Amen.

If you took that step, *congratulations!*

Everything pales in comparison to the choice to walk with Jesus through your life. Now we can apply that choice of confession to the issues in this book and to your relationships.

> Therefore **confess your sins** to each other and pray for each other so that you may be healed. The **prayer of a righteous person is powerful** and effective. (James 5:16)

Confessing your sins *to others* is not a requirement of salvation. James 5 doesn't suggest that you should confess your sins to each other so that you might be saved. Confession to God is the only path to salvation. James 5 is referring instead to healing of the mind, the mending of broken trust, and the repairing of damaged relationships that only come about by seeking forgiveness from those you have wronged in the past.

Confession clears the air and allows forgiveness to blossom where bitterness once festered. And confession carries healing power no matter what the response is. In other words, your confession starts the healing process in you, regardless of how it's received or if forgiveness is immediately granted.

◀ Work together to write a description of the purpose of confession in family relationships.

Though forgiveness in Christ is complete, sin continues to thrive in the darkness of secrecy. Confession to a loved one deflates sin's power like the air rushing out of a balloon. The sin shrivels, its grip releases, and its power dies. What was once a tool of the enemy to destroy you and your family is now a bonding agent that unites and builds strength and character. What a victory!

When is it important to confess to each other?

- When the issue is causing division
- When there is bitterness
- When you're unable to find peace
- When you need forgiveness

Now is the time to take a risk. You've confessed to God, and you're forgiven of your sins because of the death and resurrection of God's Son, Jesus. Now it's time to lay your heart bare before your loved ones. Trust that we'll get to the forgiveness part of this study just as soon as you turn the page. Let go of the fear of admitting your faults. Confess today so you can be forgiven and see your relationships restored once and for all.

Open your heart and mind, and let the Holy Spirit reveal the things that you need to let out. Let this be a safe moment in your family in which you feel free to lay your heart bare and free your spirit of any guilt or condemnation that binds you.

◀ Take this time to confess whatever the Lord is bringing to your mind. You may verbalize your confession, or write it in your own notebook or in your study guide (which you can find at www.hotbuttonsite.com).

Trust that your loved ones' response to your confession will be one of forgiveness—the next chapter will lead you through that.

Parent's Prayer

Father, I confess the times I've failed as a parent and ask You to forgive me and help me have more self-control and wisdom when I respond to things. Please help me to be a godly example and a role model for my kids. Give us the kind of relationship that mirrors the one You have with us. Thank You for Your example of unconditional love, continual acceptance, and constant approachability. Make me that kind of parent, and help my family to forgive me for the times I haven't been. Amen.

Teen's Prayer

Dear God, please forgive me for not respecting my parents all the time. Help me to honor the values we've decided upon as a family and uphold them in all things. Give me the strength to say no to the pressure I'm placed under to do all sorts of wrong things. Please help me to be a better son/daughter and make us a loving and united family that serves You together. Amen.

13 **Forgiveness**

ollowing belief and confession is forgiveness. Ah, what a blessed state to live in . . . forgiven. The very word elicits a sense of peace and calm. It inspires me to take a deep breath and rest for a moment in gratitude.

How about you? Do you feel forgiven?

> If we **confess our sins**, he is faithful and just and will **forgive us** our sins and **purify us** from all unrighteousness. (1 John 1:9)

Do you believe that you're forgiven? Sometimes it hits like a tsunami as the waves of peace wash over the heart. For others, it's more of a steady rain that takes time to feel. It's okay, either way. Whether you feel forgiven or not, you can have faith that you are, in fact, purified and holy before God.

So God has forgiven you, but now what does He expect you to do about other people who have wronged you?

> For if you **forgive other people** when they sin against you, your **heavenly Father will also forgive you**. But if you do not forgive others their sins, your Father will not forgive your sins. (Matt. 6:14–15)

◄ What does that passage teach about forgiveness?

◄ How do you feel about that?

Forgiving others is often a simple act of obedience and a step of faith. If you're angry or wronged in some way, you're rarely going to feel like forgiving those who hurt you. Forgiveness, in that case, is a gift from God planted in your heart so that you might extend it toward those who sinned against you.

Would you be surprised if I told you that offering forgiveness benefits you far more than it benefits the person you're attempting to forgive? Surrendering in that way allows God to work more deeply in your life.

◄ Read Ephesians 4:25 and Luke 15. How do you think God wants us to receive someone's confession?

◄ Now, think about this question: Can you truly accept someone's confession and offer forgiveness without holding on to any bitterness or contempt?

◄ What makes that easy or difficult for you?

◄ Read Matthew 18:21–35. Who do the characters in this parable represent? What is the debt? What is the parable trying to show us?

Bear with each another and forgive one another if any of you has a grievance against someone. **Forgive as the Lord forgave you**. And over all these virtues put on love, which binds them **all together in perfect unity**. (Col. 3:13–14)

Parents, name some times you've been forgiven of things in your life and share them here. Try for at least five examples. Spend as much time thinking about this as necessary.

When you see it written out like that, does it give you a different perspective on your teen's sins?

But I'm not God!

What about when it's just too bad, and I'm truly unable to let go of the anger toward someone?

And when you stand praying, if you hold anything against anyone, **forgive them**, so that your Father in heaven may forgive you your sins. (Mark 11:25)

Do not judge, and you will not be judged. Do not condemn, and you will not be condemned. **Forgive**, and you will be forgiven. (Luke 6:37)

Believe me, I get it. It's not easy to forgive those who have committed a painful wrong against you and are truly guilty. The problem is that unforgiveness drives a wedge into our daily walk with God. That free and open walk with a loving Savior becomes strained and even avoided when your spirit knows it's harboring something God cannot abide. He talked to His children about this specific issue because He doesn't want it to divide you from Him.

◀ Are you able to forgive each other for the things confessed before God in the last chapter? Are you able to treat those confessions with the same manner of grace that God has shown you? Is anything standing in your way? Take turns sharing.

We've made huge progress through confessing to God and each other, receiving God's grace, and forgiving others. I'd like to encourage you to backtrack a little and dig a little deeper.

◀ What are you still holding on to that needs to be confessed to your family? What sin still makes you cringe when you consider sharing it? Why can't you let it go?

Now's the time to take a chance. Forgiveness is a step away. Families, assure each other that it's safe to unload anything at this time. God has forgiven your sins, past, present, and future—now allow your family to do the same.

Confession followed by forgiveness is a life-changing gift of healing.

Parent's Prayer

Heavenly Father, I'm so grateful for Your grace and forgiveness. I'm so grateful that it extends to cover the mistakes I make as a Christian and as a parent. Please help me forgive others like You have forgiven me so that I can be an extension of Your arm of mercy to those around me. Let me show grace to my children so they will trust me with their sins and their feelings. Help me not to expect them to be perfect, but rather to see them as You see them and readily offer forgiveness at all times. Amen.

Teen's Prayer

Lord, I've done some dumb things—thank You for forgiving me for them. Your gift of salvation has changed my life, and I'm not the same person I was before You came into it. Thank You, too, for helping me and my family work through some of these things. It all makes sense when we talk about it and look at what the Bible says. Help me not to hold grudges against people who have hurt me, and help me to be obedient to You and to my parents. Please help me make good decisions and not to give in to peer pressure. Amen.

chapter 14

Clean
Slate

For as **high as the heavens** are above the earth,
so great is his love for those who fear him;
as far as the east is from the west,
so far has he **removed our transgressions** from us.
(Ps. 103:11–12)

◀ In light of Psalm 103:11–12, what does the following quote mean to you?

> "I can forgive, but I cannot forget," is only another way of saying, "I will not forgive." Forgiveness ought to be like a cancelled note, torn in two, and burned up so it can never be shown against one.   —Henry Ward Beecher

Confession + Forgiveness = Perfection   . . . *right?*

Unfortunately, I think we all know it doesn't quite work that way. The question I receive at this point in the discussion goes something like this:

"So, if I continue to mess up and the people I've forgiven continue to mess up, how can we live with a clean slate?"

◀ Read Romans 7:14–20. What does Paul do? What is he unable to do? Why is he unable to do it?

Paul is a believer. He's forgiven. He's a mighty servant of God, yet he sins. He wants to do what is right, but he often cannot. He doesn't want to do wrong, but often cannot stop himself.

◀ Continue on by reading Romans 7:21–25.

No matter how committed you are to a clean slate, your enemy, the devil, wants nothing more than to sabotage forgiveness, trust, and peace. He is the antithesis of the love you feel for each other and will stop at nothing to erode it.

There are three steps to combat the devil's attacks.

◀ Read James 4:6–8.

Step One: _____ the devil.

What does that mean to you?

What are some ways to do that as it relates to the subject of this book?

◀ Read Luke 6:27 and Acts 7:54–60.

Step Two: _____ your enemies. _____ for those who have mistreated you.

What does that mean to you?

What are some ways to do that as it relates to the issues you've been addressing with the Strategic Scenarios?

◀ Reread James 4:6–8.

Step Three: _____ _____ to God and He will _____ _____ to you.

What does that mean to you?

What are some ways to do that as it relates to the hot-button issues you've been addressing?

Immerse yourself in Scripture and prayer to counter the devil's attacks.

Romans 7 (that we looked at above) ends with a description of the battle between Paul's sin nature and his commitment to God. Good ol' Paul admits that he messes up all the time. But we know that, even though he claimed to be at war with the flesh and struggling with sin, he found favor with God. Let's take a look at Romans 8:1–4 to see the resolution:

> Therefore, **there is now no condemnation** for those who are in Christ Jesus, because through Christ Jesus the law of the Spirit who gives life has **set you free from the law of sin** and death. For what the law was powerless to do because it was weakened by the flesh, God did by **sending his own Son in the likeness of sinful flesh** to be a sin offering. And so he condemned sin in the flesh, in order that the righteous requirement of the law might be fully met in us, who do not live according to the flesh but according to the Spirit.

We have a clean slate before God. It's His promise to us in response to the work of His Son, Jesus. With the slate wiped clean for us, we are able to do the same for others. We're all a work in progress; not a single one of us is perfected and complete. We're complete in Jesus—because of Him—but not because of anything we've done. So allow others the same grace of being "in progress" that your heavenly Father is showing you by keeping your slate free from judgment.

> Being confident of this, that he who **began a good work in you** will carry it on to completion **until the day of Christ Jesus**. (Phil. 1:6)

◀ We looked at Philippians 1:6 back in chapter 1, but let's break it down again. Describe what the phrases in the verse mean to you.

Being confident of this
That He who began
A good work in you
Will carry it on to completion
Until the day of Christ Jesus

◀ How can you apply those truths to yourself and your clean slate before God?

◀ How about others and their slate before you? Is it clean in your eyes? Can you forgive an imperfect person?

From that verse, we're reminded that no one is perfect—we're all a work in progress. Commit to forgiving the failures of others, since you know that you will fail and others will forgive you.

The best way to preempt disappointment is to communicate needs and expectations. Each of you, take a moment to share three needs you have regarding the hot-button issues you've been addressing. For example: "More understanding and space when I'm in a bad mood." I recommend you put this list in writing so there's no confusion later.

Parent Commitments

Speak these commitments out loud to your teen(s):

- ◀ I commit to do my best to be a godly example.
- ◀ I commit to having an open mind and heart, ready to listen whenever you need to talk.
- ◀ I commit to being humble enough to admit when I'm wrong, but strong enough to enforce the boundaries I believe are necessary.
- ◀ I commit to _____.
  [fill in the blank based on the needs communicated above]
- ◀ I commit to _____.
  [fill in the blank based on the needs communicated above]
- ◀ I commit to _____.
  [fill in the blank based on the needs communicated above]

Sign: _____

Date: _____

Teen Commitments

Speak these commitments out loud to your parent(s):

- ◀ I commit to do my best to follow your example and do what's right, including being honest at all times.

- ◀ I commit to having an open mind to try to understand that what you ask and expect of me is for my own good.

- ◀ I commit to being humble enough to admit when I'm wrong and honest about how I feel.

- ◀ I commit to _____.
  [fill in the blank based on the needs communicated above]

- ◀ I commit to _____.
  [fill in the blank based on the needs communicated above]

- ◀ I commit to _____.
  [fill in the blank based on the needs communicated above]

Sign: _____

Date: _____

Remember that your enemy, the devil, seeks to sabotage forgiveness, trust, and peace. It's so easy to stumble down a slippery slope.

The pattern of confession, forgiveness, and a clean slate is perfectly portrayed in the relationship you have with your heavenly Father. He loves you, and wants you to walk in complete forgiveness, confident in His love for you. He also wants you to experience that love in your family.

People fail—they've failed you before, and they'll fail you again. You can't wait for God to perfect those you love, but you can allow His perfect love to cover a multitude of sins—grace from Him to you, and through you to them.

> May God himself, **the God of peace**, sanctify you through and through. May your whole spirit, soul and body **be kept blameless** at the coming of our Lord Jesus Christ. The one who calls you is faithful, and **he will do it**. (1 Thess. 5:23–24)

My Prayer for You

Heavenly Father, I lift this family up to You and thank You for their precious hearts that desire to grow closer together. Please guide them as they join hands and walk together in a united purpose to serve You throughout their lives. Facing these Hot Buttons involves release and trust. Help Mom and Dad to use wisdom in knowing when and how to begin the process of that kind of release, and help the teens to respect the boundaries set by the parents and by Your Word. Give them wisdom and strength when it comes to the choices they must make in life. Grant them Your holy sight to see down the road when the way is unclear to them. Help them also to trust each other with some of the tough decisions. As the years go by, remind them of the things they talked about in this book and the commitments they've made to each other. Give them joy as they embark on life with a clean slate. Amen.

Parent's Prayer

Father, I thank You for my family—they're perfect in Your eyes. Help me to take joy in them each and every day—just like You do. You've given us the gift of a clean slate in Your eyes . . . help us to walk in that freedom with each other too. Help me love my family like You do—unconditionally and unselfishly. Please give me wisdom and patience as I help my teens wade through these years. Amen.

Teen's Prayer

Dear Jesus, thank You for forgiveness and for a clean slate. Thank You for a family who wants to serve You and will work hard to make sure I'm on the right path. Please give me wisdom in all things, especially the choices I have to make about these hot-button issues. Help me to do the right thing and to have the strength to stand up to the pressures of life. Amen.

Recommended
Resources

Websites

www.choose-NOW.com. The Internet home of Nicole O'Dell and Choose NOW Ministries, dedicated to battling peer pressure by tackling the tough issues and bridging the gap in parent-teen communication.

http://www.focusonthefamily.com/parenting/teens/tips-for-parenting -teens.aspx. Focus on the Family is a great family-friendly resource that offers something for every aspect of parenting teens.

www.hotbuttonsite.com. The Internet home of the Hot Buttons column, where Nicole O'Dell regularly brings you new Hot Buttons scenarios free of charge, for you to use to foster healthy, proactive communication in your family.

www.susiemagazine.com. Susie Magazine is designed to focus on helping teen girls grow as well as provide them with the opportunity to connect with others, ministering to each other on a peer-to-peer level.

Books

Alcorn, Nancy. *Starved: Mercy for Eating Disorders.* Enumclaw, WA: Winepress, 2007.

Davidson, Kimberly. *I'm Beautiful? Why Can't I See It?* Mustang, OK: Tate, 2006.

Meyer, Joyce. *Battlefield of the Mind for Teens.* Nashville: Faithwords, 2006.

O'Dell, Nicole. *Girl Talk.* Uhrichsville, OH: Barbour, 2012.

Smith, Laura L. *Skinny: A Novel.* Colorado Springs: NavPress, 2008.

Notes

1. Saul McLeod, "Low Self Esteem," Simply Psychology website, 2012, http://www.simplypsychology.org/self-esteem.html.
2. Morris Rosenberg and Timothy J. Owens, "Low Self-Esteem People: A Collective Portrait." In T. J. Owens, S. Stryker, N. Goodman, eds., *Extending Self-Esteem Theory and Research* (New York: Cambridge University Press, 2001), 400–436.
3. "Self-Esteem That's Based on External Sources Has Mental Health Consequences, Study Says," *Monitor on Psychology* 33, no. 11 (December 2002), American Psychological Association website, http://www.apa.org/monitor/dec02/selfesteem.aspx.
4. Ibid.
5. Nick Vujicic, "Winning the Hand You're Dealt." *Oprah's Lifeclass.* OWN: January 20, 2012. Television.
6. Ibid.
7. Teen Anorexia Statistics, Newport Academy website, accessed May 3, 2013, http://www.newportacademy.com/anorexia-treatment/statistics/.
8. Cited in Peggy Drexler, "The Impact of Negative Body Image on Boys" in *Our Gender, Ourselves*, Psychology Today website, January 17, 2013, http://www.psychologytoday.com/blog/our-gender-ourselves/201301/the-impact-negative-body-image-boys.

9. Teen Anorexia Statistics, Newport Academy website, accessed May 3, 2013, http://www.newportacademy.com/anorexia-treatment/statistics/.

10. Ibid.

11. Bryan Miller, "How Crash Diets Harm your Health," CNNHealth, CNN, April 20, 2010, http://www.cnn.com/2010/HEALTH/04/20/crash.diets.harm.health/index.html.

12. Nigel Barber, "Daughter Has Eating Disorder: Am I a Bad Parent?" in *The Human Beast*, Psychology Today website, January 12, 2010, http://www.psychologytoday.com/blog/the-human-beast/201001/daughter-has-eating-disorder-am-i-bad-parent.

13. Victoria Rideout, "Parents, Children, & Media: A Kaiser Family Foundation Survey," Kaiser Family Foundation, June 2007, http://kaiserfamilyfoundation.files.wordpress.com/2013/01/7638.pdf.

14. Cited in Elizabeth Huebeck, "Helping Girls with Body Image," WebMD website, October 18, 2006, http://www.webmd.com/beauty/style/helping-girls-with-body-image.

About the
Author

Youth culture expert **Nicole O'Dell** resides in Paxton, Illinois, with her husband and six children—the youngest of which are preschool triplets. She is the founder of Choose NOW Ministries, dedicated to battling peer pressure and guiding teens through tough issues while helping parents encourage good decisions, and the host of *Choose NOW Radio: Parent Talk* and *Teen Talk*, where "It's all about choices!" A recent addition to the ministry, Choose HER, focuses on mother-daughter relationships.

A full-time author of both fiction and nonfiction, Nicole's desire is to bridge the gap between parents and teens. Her popular Scenarios for Girls series, the natural segue into the Hot Buttons series, asks teen readers to make tough choices for the main characters and offers alternate endings based on the individual reader's choices.

For more information on Nicole's books or to schedule her for a speaking event or interview, visit www.nicoleodell.com. Follow @Hot_Buttons on Twitter, and like www.facebook.com/HotButtons. Podcasts of *Choose NOW Radio* are available at www.chooseNOWradio.com.